THE ASSASSINS

Bernard Lewis, a world-respected authority on Islamic and Middle Eastern history, is Professor of Near Eastern Studies Emeritus at Princeton University, where he has been since 1974. Born in London in 1916, he was Professor of the History of the Middle East at the School of Oriental and African Studies, University of London, from 1949 until 1974.

Also by Bernard Lewis

The Arabs in History
The Emergence of Modern Turkey
The Muslim Discovery of Europe
Semites and Anti-Semites
The Political Language of Islam
Race and Slavery in the Middle East
The Shaping of the Modern Middle East
Cultures in Conflict: Christians, Muslims and
Jews in the Age of Discovery
The Middle East: 2000 Years of History from the
Rise of Christianity to the Present Day
The Multiple Identities of the Middle East
A Middle East Mosaic: Fragments of Life,
Letters and History
What Went Wrong?: Western Impact and
Middle Eastern Response

THE ASSASSINS

A Radical Sect in Islam

Bernard Lewis

PHOENIX

To Michael

A PHOENIX PAPERBACK

First published in Great Britain in 1967
by Weidenfeld & Nicolson
This paperback edition published in 2003
by Phoenix,
an imprint of Orion Books Ltd,
Orion House, 5 Upper St Martin's Lane,
London WC2H 9EA

Second impression 2003

Copyright © 1967 by Bernard Lewis

The right of Bernard Lewis to be identified as the
author of this work has been asserted by him in accordance
with the Copyright, Designs and Patents Act 1988.

All rights reserved. No part of this publication may be
reproduced, stored in a retrieval system, or transmitted,
in any form or by any means, electronic, mechanical,
photocopying, recording or otherwise, without the prior
permission of the copyright owner.

A CIP catalogue record for this book is
available from the British Library.

ISBN 1 84212 451 X

Printed and bound in Great Britain by
Clays Ltd, St Ives plc

Contents

Illustrations

Acknowledgements

My thanks are due to Professor J. A. Boyle and the Manchester University Press, for permission to cite a number of passages from Ata-Malik Juvaini, *The history of the world-conqueror*, translated from the Persian by John Andrew Boyle, Manchester 1958; to Professor K. M. Setton and the University of Winsconsin Press for permission to reproduce in this book some parts of my chapter on the Assassins in *A history of the Crusades*, editor-in-chief Kenneth M. Setton, vol. i, *The first hundred years*, ed. Marshall W. Baldwin, Philadelphia 1955. I would also like to express my gratitude to Mr G. Meredith-Owens, of the British Museum, for his patient and invaluable help in finding and obtaining illustrations; to Dr Nurhan Atosoy, of the University of Istanbul, for her good offices in identifying and securing copies of material in Turkish collections; to Major Peter Willey, for generously placing his photographs at my disposal; to my wife and daughter for their help in correcting the proofs; and, finally, to Professor A. T. Hatto for once again letting me profit from his keen literary judgment and acute editorial eye.   B.L.

The publishers acknowledge with thanks the permission of the following to include illustrations in this book: Major Peter Willey, plates 7, 8, 9, 10 and 11; the British Museum, plates 1 and 5; Mr S. I. Asad, plates 6 and 13; the Süleymaniye Library, Istanbul, plate 3; the Director of the Warburg Institute, plate 4; and the Topkapi Sarayi Museum, Istanbul, plate 2.

Preface to the 2003 Edition

Since this book first appeared in 1967 it has acquired a contemporary relevance which it did not have at the time of its original publication. This is perhaps indicated in its subsequent publication history. The English edition was reprinted several times both in Britain and in the United States, and a French translation in Paris appeared in 1982, with a long and interesting introduction by M. Maxime Rodinson. Three separate translations were published in Arabic, one of them with my prior knowledge and consent. An unauthorized Persian translation was published twice in Tehran, first under the monarchy, then under the republic. Translations in Japanese, Spanish, Turkish, Italian, German and Hebrew followed.

The changing nature of interest in the topic and therefore in the book is perhaps best indicated by the subtitles added by foreign translators and publishers. The English original was simply entitled *The Assassins: A Radical Sect in Islam*. In the French translation – the first foreign language version – the subtitle was changed and became 'Terrorism and Politics in Medieval Islam.' The Italian translator retained my subtitle and added 'The First Terrorists in History' – not, by the way, a correct statement. The German title was 'The Assassins: On the Tradition of Religious Murder in Radical Islam.'

The purpose of all these emendations was, clearly, to suggest a parallel between the movements and actions described in the book and those that are affecting much of the Middle East – and now also the Western world – at the present time. Certainly, the resemblance between the medieval Assassins and their modern counterparts are striking: the Syrian-Iranian connection, the calculated use of terror, the total dedication of the assassin emissary, to the point of self-immolation, in the service of his cause and in the expectation of heavenly recompense. Some have seen a further resemblance, in that both directed their attack against an external enemy, the crusaders in the one case, the Americans and the Israelis in the other.

There may indeed be such a resemblance, but if so, it is in the misapprehension rather than the reality of these attacks. According to a view widespread in the Western world since medieval times, the anger and the weapons of the Assassins were directed primarily against the Crusaders. This is simply not true. In the long list of their victims, there were very few Crusaders, and even these were marked down as the result of some internal Muslim calculation. The vast majority of their victims were Muslims, and their attacks were directed not against the outsider, seen as basically irrelevant, but against the dominant elites and prevailing ideas in the Islamic world of their time. Some modern terrorist groups do indeed focus on Israelis and on Westerners. But others, probably in the long run more important, have as their targets the existing – in their view apostate – regimes of the islamic world, and as their objective, the replacement of these regimes by a new order of their own. These points emerged very clearly from the statements made by the assassins of the Egyptian President Anwar Sadat. When the leader of the group proudly proclaimed: 'I have killed pharaoh,' he was clearly not condemning pharaoh for making peace with Israel, but as the prototype – in the Qur'an as in the Bible – of the impious tyrant.

There are also interesting resemblances and contrasts in their methods and procedures. For the medieval Assassins, the chosen victims were almost invariably the rulers and leaders of the existing order – monarchs, generals, ministers, major religious functionaries. Unlike their modern equivalents, they attacked only the great and powerful, and never harmed ordinary people going about their avocations. Their weapon was almost always the same – the dagger, wielded by the appointed Assassin in person. It is significant that they made virtually no use of such safer weapons as were available to them at the time – the bow and crossbow, missiles and poison. That is to say, they chose the most difficult and protected targets, and the most dangerous mode of attack. The Assassin himself, having struck down his assigned victim, made no attempt to escape, nor was any attempt made to rescue him. On the contrary, to have survived a mission was seen as a disgrace.

In this respect, and only in this respect, the Assassins may indeed be regarded as the forerunners of the suicide bombers of today. But in an important respect the suicide bomber marks a radical departure from earlier belief and practice. Islam has always strongly condemned suicide, regarding it as a major sin. The suicide forfeits any claim he may have had to paradise, however strong, and is doomed to eternal punishment in hell, where his torment will consist of the unending repetition of the act by which he committed suicide. A clear difference was made between throwing oneself to certain death at the hands of an overwhelmingly strong enemy, and dying by one's own hand. The first, if conducted in a properly authorized holy war, was a passport to heaven; the second to damnation. The blurring of this previously vital distinction was the work of some 20th-century Muslim theologians who outlined the new theory which the suicide bombers put into practice.

Islam, like Christianity and Judaism, is an ethical religion, and terror and blackmail have no place in its beliefs or commandments. Even while ordaining holy war as a religious duty, Islamic law lays down elaborate rules for the conduct of warfare, including such matters as the opening and termination of hostilities, the treatment of non-combatants, and the avoidance of certain indiscriminate weapons. Nevertheless, then as now, among Muslims as among others, there have been groups who practiced murder in the name of their religion, and a study of the medieval sect of Assassins may therefore serve a useful purpose – not indeed as a guide to mainstream Islamic attitudes on assassination, but as an example of how certain groups gave a radical and violent turn to the basic Islamic association of religion and politics, and tried to use it for the accomplishment of their own purposes. The story of the medieval Assassins, who appeared in Iran and spread to the Syrian and Lebanese mountains, can be instructive. And of all the lessons to be learnt from the Assassins, perhaps the most important is their final and total failure.

B.L.
Princeton, NJ
June, 2002

I

The Discovery
of the Assassins

In the year 1332, when King Philip VI of France was contemplating a new crusade to recapture the lost Holy Places of Christendom, a German priest called Brocardus composed a treatise offering the king guidance and advice for the conduct of this enterprise. Brocardus, who had spent some time in Armenia, devoted an important part of his treatise to the peculiar hazards of such an expedition to the East, and the precautions needed to guard against them. Among these dangers, said Brocardus, 'I name the Assassins, who are to be cursed and fled. They sell themselves, are thirsty for human blood, kill the innocent for a price, and care nothing for either life or salvation. Like the devil, they transfigure themselves into angels of light, by imitating the gestures, garments, languages, customs and acts of various nations and peoples; thus, hidden in sheep's clothing, they suffer death as soon as they are recognized. Since indeed I have not seen them, but know this of them only by repute or by true writings, I cannot reveal more, nor give fuller information. I cannot show how to recognize them by their customs or any other signs, for in these things they are unknown to me as to others also; nor can I show how to apprehend them by their name, for so execrable is their profession, and so abominated by all, that they conceal their own names as much as they can. I therefore know only one single remedy for the safeguarding and protection of the king, that in all the royal household, for whatever service, however small or brief or mean, none should be admitted, save those whose country, place, lineage, condition and person are certainly, fully and clearly known.'[1]

For Brocardus, the Assassins are hired, secret murderers, of a peculiarly skilful and dangerous kind. Though naming them among the hazards of the East, he does not explicitly connect them with any particular place, sect, or nation, nor ascribe any religious beliefs or political purposes to them. They are simply ruthless and competent killers, and must be guarded against as such. Indeed, by the thirteenth century, the word Assassin, in variant forms, had already passed into European usage in this general sense of hired professional murderer. The Florentine chronicler Giovanni Villani, who died in 1348, tells how the lord of Lucca sent 'his assassins' (i suoi assassini) to Pisa to kill a troublesome enemy there. Even earlier, Dante, in a passing reference in the 19th canto of the Inferno, speaks of 'the treacherous assassin' (lo perfido assassin); his fourteenth-century commentator Francesco da Buti, explaining a term which for some readers at the time may still have been strange and obscure, remarks: 'Assassino è colui che uccide altrui per danari' – An assassin is one who kills others for money.[2] Since then 'assassin' has become a common noun in most European languages. It means a murderer, more particularly one who kills by stealth or treachery, whose victim is a public figure and whose motive is fanaticism or greed.

It was not always so. The word first appears in the chronicles of the Crusades, as the name of a strange group of Muslim sectaries in the Levant, led by a mysterious figure known as the Old Man of the Mountain, and abhorrent, by their beliefs and practices, to good Christians and Muslims alike. One of the earliest descriptions of the sect occurs in the report of an envoy sent to Egypt and Syria in 1175 by the Emperor Frederick Barbarossa. 'Note', he says 'that on the confines of Damascus, Antioch and Aleppo there is a certain race of Saracens in the mountains, who in their own vernacular are called *Heyssessini*, and in Roman *segnors de montana*. This breed of men live without law; they eat swine's flesh against the law of the Saracens, and make use of all women without distinction, including their mothers and sisters. They live in the mountains and are well-nigh impregnable, for they withdraw into well-fortified castles. Their country is not very fertile, so that they live on their cattle. They have among them a Master, who strikes the greatest fear into all the Saracen princes both far and near, as well as the neighbouring Christian lords. For he has the habit of killing them in an astonishing way. The method by which this is done is as follows: this prince possesses in the mountains numerous and most beautiful palaces, surrounded by very high walls, so that none can enter except by a small and very well-guarded door. In these palaces he has many of the sons of his peasants brought up from early childhood. He has them taught various languages, as Latin, Greek, Roman, Saracen as well as many others. These young men are taught by their teachers from their earliest youth to their full manhood, that they must obey the lord of their land in all his words and commands; and that if they do so, he, who has power over all living gods, will give them the joys of paradise. They are also taught that they cannot be saved if they resist his will in anything. Note that, from the time when they are taken in as children, they see no one but their teachers and masters and receive no other instruction until they are summoned to the presence of the Prince to kill someone. When they are in the presence of the Prince, he asks them if they are willing to obey his commands, so that he may bestow paradise upon them. Whereupon, as they have been instructed, and without any objection or doubt, they throw themselves at his feet and reply with fervour, that they will obey him in all things that he may command. Thereupon the Prince gives each one of them a golden dagger and sends them out to kill whichever prince he has marked down.'

Writing a few years later, William, Archbishop of Tyre, included a brief account of the sect in his history of the Crusading states: 'There is', he said, 'in the province of Tyre, otherwise called Phoenicia, and in the diocese of Tortosa, a people who possess ten strong castles, with their dependent villages; their number, according to what we have often heard, is about 60,000 or more. It is their custom to instal their master and choose their chief, not by hereditary right, but solely by virtue of merit. Disdaining any other title of dignity, they called him the Elder.

The bond of submission and obedience that binds this people to their Chief is so strong, that there is no task so arduous, difficult or dangerous that any one of them would not undertake to perform it with the greatest zeal, as soon as the Chief has commanded it. If for example there be a prince who is hated or mistrusted by this people, the Chief gives a dagger to one or more of his followers. At once whoever receives the command sets out on his mission, without considering the consequences of the deed nor the possibility of escape. Zealous to complete his task, he toils and labours as long as may be needful, until chance gives him the opportunity to carry out his chief's orders. Both our people and the Saracens call them Assissini; we do not know the origin of this name.'[4]

In 1192 the daggers of the Assassins, which had already struck down a number of Muslim princes and officers, found their first Crusader victim – Conrad of Montferrat, king of the Latin Kingdom of Jerusalem. This murder made a profound impression among the Crusaders, and most of the chroniclers of the Third Crusade have something to say about the dreaded sectaries, their strange beliefs, their terrible methods, and their redoubtable chief. 'I shall now relate things about this elder', says the German chronicler Arnold of Lübeck, 'which appear ridiculous, but which are attested to me by the evidence of reliable witnesses. This Old Man has by his witchcraft so bemused the men of his country, that they neither worship nor believe in any God but himself. Likewise he entices them in a strange manner with such hopes and with promises of such pleasures with eternal enjoyment, that they prefer rather to die than to live. Many of them even, when standing on a high wall, will jump off at his nod or command, and, shattering their skulls, die a miserable death. The most blessed, so he affirms, are those who shed the blood of men and in revenge for such deeds themselves suffer death. When therefore any of them have chosen to die in this way, murdering someone by craft and then themselves dying so blessedly in revenge for him, he himself hands them knives which are, so to speak, consecrated to this affair, and then intoxicates them with such a potion that they are plunged into ecstasy and oblivion, displays to them by his magic certain fantastic dreams, full of pleasures and delights, or rather of trumpery, and promises them eternal possession of these things in reward for such deeds.'[5]

At first it was the fanatical devotion, rather than the murderous methods, of the Assassins that struck the imagination of Europe. 'You have me more fully in your power', says a Provençal troubadour to his lady, than 'the Old Man has his Assassins, who go to kill his mortal enemies . . .' 'Just as the Assassins serve their master unfailingly,' says another, 'so I have served Love with unswerving loyalty.' In an anonymous love-letter, the writer assures his lady: 'I am your Assassin, who hopes to win paradise through doing your commands.'[6] In time, however, it was murder, rather than loyalty, that made the more powerful impression, and gave the word assassin the meaning that it has retained to the present day.

As the stay of the Crusaders in the Levant lengthened, more information about the Assassins became available, and there were even some Europeans who met and talked with them. The Templars and Hospitallers succeeded in establishing an ascendancy over the Assassin castles, and collected tribute from them. William of Tyre records an abortive approach by the Old Man of the Mountain to the King of Jerusalem, proposing some form of alliance; his continuator relates a somewhat questionable story of how Count Henry of Champagne, returning from Armenia in 1198, was entertained in his castle by the Old Man, who ordered a number of his henchmen to leap to their deaths from the ramparts for the edification of his guest, and then hospitably offered to provide others for his requirements: 'and if there was any man who had done him an injury, he should let him know, and he would have him killed.' Somewhat more plausibly, the English historian Matthew of Paris reports the arrival in Europe in 1238 of an embassy from some Muslim rulers, 'and principally from the Old Man of the Mountain'; they had come to seek help from the French and the English against the new, looming menace of the Mongols from the East. By 1250, when St Louis led a crusade to the Holy Land, it was possible for him to exchange gifts and missions with the Old Man of the Mountain of that time. An

Arabic-speaking friar, Yves the Breton, accompanied the king's messengers to the Assassins, and discussed religion with their chief. In his account, through the mists of ignorance and prejudice, one can faintly discern some of the known doctrines of the Islamic sect to which the Assassins belonged.[7]

The Crusaders knew the Assassins only as a sect in Syria, and show little or no awareness of their place in Islam, or their connections with other groups elsewhere in the Muslim lands. One of the best informed of crusading writers on Muslim affairs, James of Vitry, bishop of Acre, noted at the beginning of the thirteenth century that the sect had begun in Persia – but seems to have known no more than that.[8] In the second half of the century, however, new and direct information appeared concerning the parent sect in Persia. The first informant was William of Rubruck, a Flemish priest sent on a mission by the King of France to the court of the Great Khan at Karakorum in Mongolia, in the years 1253–5. William's journey took him through Persia where, he notes, the mountains of the Assassins adjoin the Caspian mountains south of the Caspian sea. At Karakorum William was struck by the elaborate security precautions, the reason for which was that the Great Khan had heard that no less than forty Assassins, in various disguises, had been sent to murder him. In response he sent one of his brothers with an army against the land of the Assassins, and ordered him to kill them all.[9]

The word William uses for the Assassins in Persia is Muliech or Mulihet – a corruption of the Arabic *mulḥid*, plural *malāḥida*. This word, literally meaning deviator, was commonly applied to deviant religious sects, and particularly to the Ismailis, the group to which the Assassins belonged. It appears again in the account of a very much more famous traveller, Marco Polo, who passed through Persia in 1273, and describes the fortress and valley of Alamut, for long the headquarters of the sect.

'The Old Man was called in their language ALOADIN. He had caused a certain valley between two mountains to be enclosed, and had turned it into a garden, the largest and most beautiful that ever was seen, filled with every variety of fruit. In it were erected pavilions and palaces the most elegant that can be imagined, all covered with gilding and exquisite painting. And there were runnels too, flowing freely with wine and milk and honey and water; and numbers of ladies and of the the most beautiful damsels in the world, who could play on all manner of instruments, and sung [sic] most sweetly, and danced in a manner that it was charming to behold. For the Old Man desired to make his people believe that this was actually Paradise. So he had fashioned it after the description that Mahommet gave of his Paradise, to wit, that it should be a beautiful garden running with conduits of wine and milk and honey and water, and full of lovely women for the delectation of all its inmates. And sure enough the Saracens of those parts believed that it *was* Paradise!

'Now no man was allowed to enter the Garden save those whom he intended to be his ASHISHIN. There was a Fortress at the entrance to the Garden, strong enough to resist all the world, and there was no other way to get in. He kept at his Court a number of the youths of the country, from twelve to twenty years of age, such as had a taste for soldiering, and to these he used to tell tales about Paradise, just as Mahommet had been wont to do, and they believed in him just as the Saracens believe in Mahommet. Then he would introduce them into his garden, some four, or six, or ten at a time, having first made them drink a certain potion which cast them into a deep sleep, and then causing them to be lifted and carried in. So when they awoke, they found themselves in the Garden.

'When therefore they awoke, and found themselves in a place so charming, they deemed that it was Paradise in very truth. And the ladies and damsels dallied with them to their hearts' content, so that they had what young men would have; and with their own good will they never would have quitted the place.

'Now this Prince whom we call the Old One kept his Court in grand and noble style, and made those simple hill-folks about him believe firmly that he was a great prophet. And when he wanted one of his *Ashishin* to send on any mission, he would cause that potion whereof I spoke to be given to one of the youths in the garden, and then had him carried into his Palace. So when the young man awoke, he found himself in the Castle, and no longer in that Paradise; whereat he was not over well pleased. He was then conducted to the Old Man's presence, and bowed before him with great veneration as believing himself to be in the presence of a true prophet. The Prince would then ask whence he came, and he would reply that he came from Paradise! and that it was exactly such as Mahommet had described it in the Law. This of course gave the others who stood by, and who had not been admitted, the greatest desire to enter therein.

'So when the Old Man would have any Prince slain, he would say to such a youth: "Go thou and slay So and So; and when thou returnest my angels shall bear thee into Paradise. And should'st thou die, nevertheless even so will I send my Angels to carry thee back into Paradise." So he caused them to believe; and thus there was no order of his that they would not affront any peril to execute, for the great desire they had to get back into that Paradise of his. And in this manner the Old One got his people to murder any one whom he desired to get rid of. Thus, too, the great dread that he inspired all Princes withal, made them become his tributaries in order that he might abide at peace and amity with them.

'I should also tell you that the Old Man had certain others under him, who copied his proceedings and acted exactly in the same manner. One of these was sent into the territory of Damascus, and the other into Curdistan.'[10]

In speaking of the Ismailis of Persia as Assassins, and of their leader as the Old Man, Marco Polo – or his transcriber – was using terms already familiar in Europe. They had, however, come from Syria, not from Persia. The Arabic and Persian sources make it quite clear that 'Assassin' was a local name, applied only to the Ismailis of Syria, and never to those of Persia or any other country.[11] The title 'Old Man of the Mountain' was also Syrian. It would be natural for the Ismailis to speak of their chief as Old Man or Elder, Arabic *Shaykh* or Persian *Pīr*, a common term of respect among Muslims. The specific designation 'Old Man of the Mountain', however, seems to have been used only in Syria, and perhaps only among the Crusaders, since it has not yet come to light in any Arabic text of the period.

The use of these terms, for both the Syrian and Persian branches of the sect, became general. Marco Polo's description, followed some half century later by a similar account from Odoric of Pordenone, deepened the impact which the Syrian Assassins had made on the imagination of Europe. The stories of the gardens of paradise, the death-leap of the devotees, the superlative skill of the Assassins in disguise and in murder, and the mysterious figure of their chief, the Old Man of the Mountain, find many echoes in the literatures of Europe, spreading from history and travel into poetry, fiction, and myth.

They had their effect on politics also. From quite an early date there were some who detected the hand of the Old Man in political murders or attempts at murder even in Europe. In 1158, when Frederick Barbarossa was besieging Milan, an 'Assassin' was allegedly caught in his camp; in 1195, when King Richard Coeur de Lion was at Chinon, no less than fifteen so-called Assassins were apprehended, and confessed that they had been sent by the King of France to kill him. Before long, such charges became frequent, and numerous rulers or leaders were accused of being in league with the Old Man and of employing the services of his emissaries to destroy an inconvenient enemy. There can be little doubt that these charges are baseless. The chiefs of the Assassins, in Persia or in Syria, had no interest in the plots and intrigues of Western Europe; the European needed no help from outside in the various arts of murder. By the fourteenth century, the word assassin had come to mean murderer, and no longer implied any specific connection with the sect to which that name had originally belonged.

The sect continued however to arouse interest. The first Western attempt at a scholarly investigation of their history seems to be that of Denis Lebey de Batilly, published in Lyons in 1603. The date is significant. The pagan ethics of the Renaissance had brought a revival of murder as an instrument of policy; the wars of religion had elevated it to a pious duty. The emergence of the new monarchies, in which one man could determine the politics and religion of the state, made assassination an effective as well as an acceptable weapon. Princes and prelates were willing to hire murderers to strike down their political or religious opponents – and theorists were forthcoming to clothe the naked logic of violence in a decent covering of ideology.

Lebey de Batilly's purpose was modest; to explain the true historic meaning of a term which had acquired new currency in France. His study is based exclusively on Christian sources, and does not therefore go much beyond what was known in Europe in the thirteenth century. But even without new evidence there could be new insights. These must have come easily to the generation that had seen William of Nassau shot by a hireling of the King of Spain, Henry III of France stabbed by a Dominican friar, and Elizabeth of England hard pressed to escape her consecrated would-be murderers.

The first really important advance towards solving the mystery of Assassin origins and identity was a product of the early Enlightenment. It came in 1697, with the publication of Bartholomé d'Herbelot's great *Bibliothèque orientale*, a pioneer work containing most of what orientalist scholarship in Europe could at that time offer on the history, religion and literature of Islam. Here for the first time an enquiring and undogmatic Western scholar made use of Muslim sources – the few that were then known in Europe – and tried to situate the Persian and Syrian Assassins in the broader context of Islamic religious history. They belonged, he showed, to the Ismailis, an important dissident sect, and itself an off-shoot of the Shi'a, whose quarrel with the Sunnis was the major religious schism in Islam. The heads of the Ismaili sect claimed to be Imams, descendants of Isma'il ibn Ja'far, and through him of the Prophet Muhammad by his daughter Fatima and his son-in-law Ali. During the eighteenth century other orientalists and historians took up the theme, and added new details on the history, beliefs and connections of the Assassins and their parent sect, the Ismailis. Some writers also tried to explain the origin of the name Assassin – a word generally assumed to be Arabic, but not as yet attested in any known Arabic text. Several etymologies were proposed, none of them very convincing.

The beginning of the nineteenth century saw a new burst of

interest in the Assassins. The French Revolution and its after-math had revived public interest in conspiracy and murder; Bonaparte's expedition to Egypt and Syria brought new and closer contacts with the Islamic orient, and new opportunities for Islamic studies. After some attempts by lesser men to satisfy public interest, Silvestre de Sacy, the greatest Arabic scholar of the time, turned his attention to the theme, and on 19 May 1809 read a memoir to the *Institut de France*, on the dynasty of the Assassins and the etymology of their name.[12]

Silvestre de Sacy's memoir was a landmark in Assassin studies. In addition to the handful of oriental sources used by previous scholars, he was able to draw on a rich collection of Arabic manuscripts in the *Bibliothèque Nationale* in Paris, including several of the major Arabic chronicles of the Crusades hitherto unknown to Western scholarship; his analysis of the sources wholly superseded the efforts of earlier European writers. Certainly the most important part of the memoir was his solution, once and for all, of the vexed problem of the origin of the word 'Assassin'. After examining and dismissing previous theories, he showed conclusively that the word came from the Arabic *hashīsh*, and suggested that the variant forms Assassini, Assissini, Heyssisini etc. in the crusading sources were based on the alternative Arabic forms *hashīshī* and *hashshāsh* (colloquial plurals, *hashīshiyyīn* and *hashshāshīn*). In confirmation of this he was able to adduce several Arabic texts in which the sectaries were called *hashīshī*, but none in which they were called *hashshāsh* Since then, the form *hashīshī* has been confirmed by additional texts that have come to light – but there is still, as far as is known, no text in which the Ismailis are called *hashshāsh*. It would therefore seem that this part of Silvestre de Sacy's explanation must be abandoned, and all the European variants derived from the Arabic *hashīshī* and its plural *hashīshiyyīn*.

This revision raises again the question of the significance, as distinct from the etymology, of the term. The original meaning of *hashīsh* in Arabic is herbage, more particularly dry herbage or fodder. Later it was specialized to denote Indian hemp, *cannabis sativa*, the narcotic effects of which were already known to the

Muslims in the Middle Ages. *Ḥashshāsh*, a more modern word, is the common term for a hashish-taker. Silvestre de Sacy, while not adopting the opinion held by many later writers that the Assassins were so called because they were addicts, nevertheless explains the name as due to the secret use of hashish by the leaders of the sect, to give their emissaries a foretaste of the delights of paradise that awaited them on the successful completion of their missions. He links this interpretation with the story told by Marco Polo, and also found in other eastern and western sources, of the secret 'gardens of paradise' into which the drugged devotees were introduced.

Despite its early appearance and wide currency, this story is almost certainly untrue. The use and effects of hashish were known at the time, and were no secret; the use of the drug by the sectaries is attested neither by Ismaili nor by serious Sunni authors. Even the name *ḥashīshī* is local to Syria, and is probably a term of popular abuse. In all probability it was the name that gave rise to the story, rather than the reverse. Of various explanations that have been offered, the likeliest is that it was an expression of contempt for the wild beliefs and extravagant behaviour of the sectaries – a derisive comment on their conduct rather than a description of their practices. For Western observers in particular, such stories may also have served to provide a rational explanation for behaviour that was otherwise totally inexplicable.

Silvestre de Sacy's memoir opened the way for a series of further studies on the subject. Certainly the most widely read of these was the *History of the Assassins* of the Austrian orientalist Joseph von Hammer, published in German in Stuttgart in 1818 and in French and English translations in 1833 and 1835. Hammer's history, though based on oriental sources, is very much a tract for the times – a warning against 'the pernicious influence of secret societies ... and ... the dreadful prostitution of religion to the horrors of unbridled ambition'. For him, the Assassins were a 'union of impostors and dupes which, under the mask of a more austere creed and severer morals, undermined all religion and morality; that order of murderers, beneath whose daggers the lords of nations fell; all powerful, because, for the space of three centuries, they were universally dreaded, until the den of ruffians fell with the khaliphate, to whom, as the centre of spiritual and temporal power, it had at the outset sworn destruction, and by whose ruins it was itself overwhelmed'. In case any of his readers miss the point, Hammer compares the Assassins with the Templars, the Jesuits, the Illuminati, the Freemasons, and the regicides of the French National Convention. 'As in the west, revolutionary societies arose from the bosom of the Freemasons, so in the east, did the Assassins spring from the Ismailites ... The insanity of the enlighteners, who thought that by mere preaching, they could emancipate nations from the protecting care of princes, and the leading-strings of practical religion, has shown itself in the most terrible manner by the effects of the French revolution, as it did in Asia, in the reign of Hassan II.'[13]

Hammer's book exercised considerable influence, and for about a century and a half was the main source of the popular Western image of the Assassins. Meanwhile scholarly research was progressing, especially in France, where much work was done in discovering, editing, translating and exploiting Arabic and Persian texts relating to the history of the Ismailis in Syria and Persia. Among the most important were the works of two Persian historians of the Mongol period, Juvayni and Rashid al-Din; both of them had access to Ismaili writings from Alamut, and, by using them, were able to provide the first connected account of the Ismaili principality in Northern Persia.

An important step forward was made possible by the appearance of material of a new kind. The use of Muslim sources had added much to the knowledge derived from mediaeval European works – but even these were mainly Sunni; though far better informed than the Western chroniclers and travellers, they were if anything even more hostile to the doctrines and purposes of the Ismailis. Now, for the first time, information came to light which reflected directly the point of view of the Ismailis themselves. Already in the eighteenth century travellers had noted that there were still Ismailis in some villages in Central Syria. In 1810 Rousseau, the French consul-general in Aleppo, stimulated by Silvestre de Sacy, published a description of the Ismailis in

Syria in his own day, with geographical, historical, and religious data.[14] The sources are not given, but appear to be local and oral. Silvestre de Sacy himself provided some additional explanatory notes. Rousseau was the first European to draw on such local informants, bringing to Europe for the first time some scraps of information from the Ismailis themselves. In 1812 he published extracts from an Ismaili book obtained in Masyaf, one of the main Ismaili centres in Syria. Though it contains little historical information, it throws some light on the religious doctrines of the sect. Other texts from Syria also found their way to Paris, where some of them were later published. During the nineteenth century a number of European and American travellers visited the Ismaili villages in Syria, and reported briefly on the ruins and their inhabitants.

Less information was available from Persia, where the remains of the great castle of Alamut still stand. In 1833, in the *Journal of the Royal Geographical Society*, a British officer called Colonel W. Monteith described a journey in which he had got as far as the entrance to the Alamut valley but did not actually reach or identify the castle. This was achieved by a brother officer, Lieutenant-Colonel [Sir] Justin Sheil, whose account appeared in the same journal in 1838. A third British officer, named Stewart, visited the castle a few years later, after which nearly a century passed before the exploration of Alamut was resumed.[15]

But there were more than ruins to commemorate the past greatness of the Ismailis in Persia. In 1811, Consul Rousseau from Aleppo, in the course of a journey to Persia, enquired about Ismailis, and was surprised to learn that there were still many in the country who owed allegiance to an Imam of the line of Ismail. His name was Shah Khalilullah, and he resided in a village called Kehk, near Qumm, half-way between Tehran and Isfahan. 'I may add,' says Rousseau, 'that Shah Khalilullah is revered almost as a god by his followers, who attribute the gift of miracles to him, enrich him continually with what they bequeath, and often embellish him with the pompous title of Caliph. There are Ismailis as far away as India, and they can be seen regularly coming to Kehk from the banks of the Ganges and the Indus, to receive the blessings of their Imam, in return for the pious and magnificent offerings which they bring him.'[16]

In 1825 an English traveller, J. B. Fraser, confirmed the survival of Ismailis in Persia, and their continued devotion to their chief, though they no longer practised murder at his behest: 'even at this day the sheikh or head of the sect is most blindly revered by those who yet remain, though their zeal has lost the deep and terrific character which it once bore.' There were followers of the sect in India too, who were 'particularly devoted to their saint'. Their previous chief, Shah Khalilullah, had been murdered in Yazd some years earlier (in fact in 1817), by rebels against the governor of the city. 'He was succeeded in his religious capacity by one of his sons, who meets with a similar respect from the sect.'[17]

The next accession of information came from quite a different source. In December 1850, a somewhat unusual case of murder came before the criminal court in Bombay. Four men had been set upon and murdered, in broad daylight, as the result of a difference of opinion within the religious community to which they belonged. Nineteen men were tried, and four of them were sentenced to death and hanged. The victims and their attackers were both members of a local Muslim sect known as the Khojas – a community of some tens of thousands, mainly traders, in the Bombay Presidency and other parts of India.

The incident arose from a dispute that had been going on for more than twenty years. It had begun in 1827, when a group of Khojas had refused to make the customary payments to the head of their sect, who resided in Persia. This was the son of Shah Khalilullah, who had succeeded his murdered father in 1817. In 1818 the Shah of Persia had appointed him governor of Mehellat and Qumm, and had given him the title of Aga Khan. It is by this title that he and his descendants are usually known.

Confronted with this sudden refusal by a group of his followers in India to pay their religious dues, the Aga Khan sent a special envoy from Persia to Bombay, to bring them back into the fold. With the envoy went the Aga Khan's grandmother, who 'herself appears to have harangued the Bombay Khojas' in an effort to regain their allegiance. Most of the Khojas remained faithful to their chief, but a small group persisted in their opposition, maintaining that they owed no obedience to the Aga Khan and denying that the Khojas were in any way connected with him. The resulting conflicts aroused strong feelings in the community and culminated in the murders of 1850.

In the meantime the Aga Khan himself had left Persia, where he had led an unsuccessful rising against the Shah, and after a short stay in Afghanistan he had taken refuge in India. His services to the British in Afghanistan and Sind gave him some claim to British gratitude. After staying first in Sind and then in Calcutta, he finally settled in Bombay, where he established himself as effective head of the Khoja community. There were still, however, some dissidents who opposed him, and who sought to use the machinery of the law to defeat his claims. After some preliminary actions, in April 1866 a group of seceders filed information and a bill in the High Court of Bombay, asking for an injunction restraining the Aga Khan 'from interfering in the management of the trust property and affairs of the Khoja community'.

The case was tried by the Chief Justice, Sir Joseph Arnould. The hearing lasted for 25 days, and involved almost the whole of the Bombay bar. Both sides brought elaborately argued and extensively documented cases, and the enquiries of the court ranged far and deep, in history and genealogy, theology and law. Among numerous witnesses, the Aga Khan himself testified before the court, and adduced evidence of his descent. On 12 November 1866 Sir Joseph Arnould delivered judgement. The Khojas of Bombay, he found, were part of the larger Khoja community of India, whose religion was that of the Ismaili wing of the Shi'a; they were 'a sect of people whose ancestors were Hindu in origin; which was converted to and has throughout abided in the faith of the Shia Imamee Ismailis; which has always been and still is bound by ties of spiritual allegiance to the hereditary Imams of the Ismailis'. They had been converted some four hundred years previously by an Ismaili missionary from Persia, and had remained subject to the spiritual authority of the line of Ismaili Imams, the latest of whom was the Aga Khan. These Imams were descended from the Lords of Alamut, and, through them, claimed descent from the Fatimid Caliphs of Egypt and, ultimately, from the Prophet Muhammad. Their followers, in mediaeval times, had become famous under the name of the Assassins.

The Arnould judgement, supported by a wealth of historical evidence and argument, thus legally established the status of the Khojas as a community of Ismailis, of the Ismailis as heirs of the Assassins, and of the Aga Khan as spiritual head of the Ismailis and heir of the Imams of Alamut. Detailed information about the community was provided for the first time in the *Gazetteer of the Bombay Presidency* in 1899.[18]

The Arnould judgement had also drawn attention to the existence of Ismaili communities in other parts of the world, some of which did not in fact recognize the Aga Khan as their chief. These communities were usually small minorities in remote and isolated places, difficult of access in every sense, and secretive to the point of death about their beliefs and their writings. Some of these writings, in manuscript, nevertheless found their way into the hands of scholars. At first these all came from Syria – the first area of Western interest in the Ismailis, in modern as in mediaeval times. Others followed, from widely separated regions. In 1903 an Italian merchant called Caprotti brought a collection of some sixty Arabic manuscripts from San'a, in the Yemen – the first of several batches which were deposited in the Ambrosiana library in Milan. On inspection, they were found to include several works on Ismaili doctrine, coming from among the Ismaili population still living in parts of Southern Arabia. Some of them contained passages written in secret cyphers.[19] At the other end of Europe, Russian scholars, who had already received some Ismaili manuscripts from Syria, discovered that they had Ismailis within the frontiers of their own Empire, and in 1902 Count Alexis Bobrinskoy published an account of the organization and distribution of the Ismailis in Russian Central Asia. At about the same time a colonial official called A. Polovtsev acquired a copy of an Ismaili religious book, written in Persian; it was deposited in the Asiatic Museum of the Imperial Russian Academy of the Sciences. Another copy followed, and between 1914 and 1918 the Museum acquired a collection of Ismaili manuscripts, brought from Shughnan, on the upper Oxus river, by the orientalists I. I. Zarubin and A. A. Semyonov. With these, and other subsequently acquired manuscripts, Russian scholars were able to examine the religious literature and beliefs of the Ismailis of the Pamir and of the adjoining Afghan districts of Badakhshan.[20]

Since then, the progress of Ismaili studies has been rapid and remarkable. Many more Ismaili texts have become available, especially from the rich libraries of the sect in the Indian sub-continent, and much detailed research has been produced by scholars in many lands, including some who are themselves Ismailis. In one respect the recovery of the lost literature of the sect has been somewhat disappointing – in history. The books that have come to light are concerned almost exclusively with religion and related matters; works of an historical nature are both few in number and poor in content – perhaps inevitably in a minority community which possessed neither the territorial nor the institutional focus about which alone the mediaeval historian could conceive and write history. Only the principality of Alamut seems to have had its chronicles – and even these are preserved by Sunni, not Ismaili historians. But Ismaili literature, though poor in historical content, is by no means lacking in historical value. Its contribution to the narrative history of events is small – something on the Assassins of Persia, rather less on their brothers in Syria. It has however contributed immeasurably to the better understanding of the religious background of the movement, and has made possible a new appreciation of the beliefs and purposes, the religious and historical significance of the Ismailis in Islam, and of the Assassins as a branch of the Ismailis. The resulting picture of the Assassins differs radically both from the lurid rumours and fantasies brought back from the East by mediaeval travellers, and from the hostile and distorted image extracted by nineteenth-century orientalists from the manuscript writings of orthodox Muslim theologians and historians, whose main concern was to refute and condemn, not to understand or explain. The Assassins no longer appear as a gang of drugged dupes led by scheming impostors, as a conspiracy of nihilistic terrorists, or as a syndicate of professional murderers. They are no less interesting for that.

2

The Ismailis

The first crisis in Islam came at the death of the Prophet in 632. Muhammad had never claimed to be more than a mortal man – distinguished above others because he was God's messenger and the bearer of God's word, but himself neither divine nor immortal. He had, however, left no clear instructions on who was to succeed him as leader of the Islamic community and ruler of the nascent Islamic state, and the Muslims had only the meagre political experience of pre-Islamic Arabia to guide them. After some arguments and a moment of dangerous tension, they agreed to appoint Abu Bakr, one of the earliest and most respected converts, as *khalīfa*, deputy, of the Prophet – thus creating, almost incidentally, the great historical institution of the Caliphate.

From the first days of the Caliphate there was a group of people who felt that Ali, the cousin and son-in-law of the Prophet, had a stronger claim to his succession than Abu Bakr or the Caliphs who followed him. In part no doubt their support for Ali was due to the conviction that his personal qualities made him the best man for the job – in part perhaps also to a legitimist belief in the rights of the house of the Prophet. This group came to be known as the *Shi'atu 'Alī*, the party of Ali, and then simply as the *Shī'a*. In the course of time it gave rise to the most important religious conflict in Islam.

At first, the Shi'a was primarily a political faction – the supporters of a candidate for power, with no distinctive religious doctrines and no greater religious content than was inherent in the very nature of Islamic political authority. But soon important changes occurred both in the composition of its following and the nature of its teachings. To many Muslims it seemed that the Islamic community and state had taken a wrong turning; instead of the ideal society envisaged by the Prophet and his first, pious Companions, an Empire had come into being, ruled by a greedy and unscrupulous aristocracy; instead of justice and equality, there was inequality, privilege and domination. To many who saw events in this light, it seemed that a return to the kin of the Prophet might bring a restoration of the true, original message of Islam.

In the year 656, after the murder by Muslim mutineers of the third Caliph Uthman, Ali finally became Caliph – but his reign was brief, and marred by dissension and civil war. When he in turn was murdered in 661, the Caliphate passed into the hands of his rival Mu'awiya, whose family, the house of Umayya, retained it for nearly a century.

The *Shi'a* of Ali did not disappear with his death. Significant groups of Muslims continued to give their allegiance to the kin of the Prophet, in whom they saw the rightful leaders of the Muslim community. Increasingly, these claims, and the support which they evoked, acquired a religious, even a messianic character. The Muslim state, ideally conceived, is a religious polity, established and maintained under divine law. Its sovereignty derives from God; its sovereign, the Caliph, is entrusted with the duties of upholding Islam and of enabling Muslims to live the good Muslim life. In this society the distinction between secular and religious is unknown – in law, in jurisdiction, or in authority. Church and state are one and the same, with the Caliph as head. Where the basis of identity and cohesion in society, the bonds of loyalty and duty in the state, are all conceived and expressed in religious terms, the familiar Western distinction between religion and politics – between religious and political attitudes and activities – becomes irrelevant and unreal. Political dissatisfaction – itself perhaps socially determined – finds religious expression; religious dissent acquires political implications. When a group of Muslims offered more than purely local or personal opposition to the men in power – when they formulated a challenge to the existing order and formed an organization to change it, their challenge was a theology and their organization a sect. In the theocratically conceived Islamic order of the Caliphate, there was no other way for them to forge an instrument or formulate a doctrine going beyond their personal actions and their immediate aims.

In the first century of Islamic expansion there were many tensions that gave rise to grievances, many grievances and aspirations that found expression in sectarian dissent and revolt. The spread of Islam by conversion brought into the Islamic community large numbers of new believers, who carried with them, from their Christian, Jewish and Iranian backgrounds, religious concepts and attitudes unknown to the early Arab Muslims. These new converts, though Muslims, were not Arabs, still less aristocrats; the inferior social and economic status assigned to them by the dominant Arab aristocracy created a sense of injustice, and made them willing recruits to movements that questioned the legitimacy of the existing order. Nor were the Arab conquerors themselves immune to these discontents. Pious Arabs deplored the worldliness of the Caliphs and the ruling groups; nomadic Arabs resented the encroachments of authority – and many others, who suffered from the sharper economic and social differences that came with conquest and riches, began to share the griefs and hopes of the new converts. Many of these had traditions of political and religious legitimism – the Jewish and Christian belief in the sanctity and ultimate triumph of the royal house of David, through the anointed Messiah, the Zoroastrian expectation of a Saoshyans, a saviour who would arise at the end of time from the holy seed of Zoroaster. Once converted to Islam, they were readily attracted by the claims of the house of the Prophet, which seemed to offer an end to the inequities of the existing order and the fulfilment of the promise of Islam.

In the transformation of the Shi'a from a party to a sect, two events are of special significance, both of them arising from unsuccessful attempts by Shi'ite claimants to overthrow the Umayyad Caliphate. The first, in the year 680, was led by Husayn, the son of Ali and his wife Fatima, the daughter of the Prophet. On the tenth day of the month of Muharram, at a place called Karbala in Iraq, Husayn, his family, and his followers encountered an Umayyad force and were ruthlessly put to death. Some seventy died in the massacre; only a sick boy, Ali ibn Husayn, who was left lying in a tent, survived. This dramatic martyrdom of the kin of the Prophet, and the wave of anguish and penitence that followed it, infused a new religious fervour in the Shi'a, now inspired by the potent themes of suffering, passion and expiation.

A second turning point came at the end of the seventh and beginning of the eighth century. In 685, one Mukhtar, an Arab of Kufa, led a revolt in the name of a son of Ali known as Muhammad ibn al-Hanafiyya, who was, he said, the Imam, the true and rightful head of the Muslims. Mukhtar was defeated and killed in 687, but his movement survived. When Muhammad ibn al-Hanafiyya himself died in about 700, there were some who said that the Imamate had passed to his son. Others claimed that he was not really dead, but had gone into hiding in the mountains of Radwa, near Mecca; from there, in God's good time, he would return and triumph over his enemies. Such a messianic Imam is called the *Mahdi*, the rightly-guided one.

These events set the pattern for a long series of religious re-volutionary movements. There are two central figures in such a movement: the Imam, who is sometimes also the Mahdi, the rightful leader who comes to destroy tyranny and establish justice, and the *dā'ī*, the summoner, who preaches – and often also devises – his message, enlists his disciples, and finally, it may be, leads them to victory or martyrdom. In the middle of the eighth century one of these movements even won a transitory success, bringing about the overthrow of the Umayyads and their re-placement by the Abbasids, another branch of the family to which both the Prophet and Ali had belonged – but in the hour of their triumph the Abbasid Caliphs renounced the sect and da'is that had brought them to power, and chose the path of stability and continuity in religion and politics. The resulting frustration of revolutionary hopes gave rise to new and fierce discontents, and a new wave of extremist and messianic movements.

In early times both the doctrines and organizations of the Shi'a were subject to frequent variation. Numerous pretenders appeared, claiming, with varying plausibility, to be members or agents of the house of the Prophet and, after enriching the mythical description of the awaited redeemer with some new detail, disappeared from human eyes. Their programmes varied from moderate, more or less dynastic opposition to extreme religious heterodoxy, far removed from the commonly accepted teachings of Islam. A recurring feature is the cult of holy men – Imams and da'is – who were believed to possess miraculous powers, and whose doctrines reflect mystical and illuminationist ideas derived from Gnosticism, Manichaeism, and various Iranian and Judaeo-Christian heresies. Among the beliefs attributed to them are those of reincarnation, the deification of the Imams and sometimes even of the da'is, and libertinism – the abandonment of all law and restraint. In some areas – as for example among the peasants and nomads in parts of Persia and Syria – distinctive local religions emerged, resulting from the interaction of Shi'ite teachings and earlier local cults and creeds.

The political programme of the sects was obvious: to overthrow the existing order and instal their chosen Imam. It is more difficult to identify any social or economic programme, though their activities were clearly related to social and economic discontents and aspirations. Some idea of these aspirations may be inferred from the messianic traditions that were current, showing what needs the Mahdi was expected to meet. Part of his task was, in the broad sense, Islamic – to restore the true Islam, and spread the faith to the ends of the earth. More specifically, he was to bring justice – to 'fill the world with justice and equity as it is now filled with tyranny and oppression', to establish equality between the weak and the strong, and to bring peace and plenty.

At first, the leaders to whom the Shi'a gave their allegiance based their claims on kinship with the Prophet rather than on descent from him in the direct line, through his daughter Fatima; some of them, including a few of the most active, were not descendants of Fatima – some not even of Ali, but of other branches of the Prophet's clan. But after the victory and betrayal of the Abbasids, the Shi'a concentrated their hopes on the descendants of Ali and, among these, more particularly on those who sprang from his marriage with the Prophet's daughter. Increasing stress was laid on the importance of direct descent from the Prophet, and the idea gained ground that since the Prophet's death there had in fact been a single line of legitimate Imams, who alone were the rightful heads of the Islamic community. These were Ali, his sons Hasan and Husayn, and the descendants of Husayn through his son Ali Zayn al-Abidin, the solitary survivor of the tragedy at Karbala. Apart from Husayn, these Imams had in the main refrained from political activity. While other claimants spent themselves in vain attempts to overthrow the Caliphate by force, the legitimate Imams preferred to function as a sort of legal opposition to the Caliphs in power. They resided in Mecca or Medina, far from the main political centres, and, while maintaining their claims, did little to advance them. On the contrary, they sometimes gave recognition, and even help and advice to the Umayyad, and after them to the Abbasid rulers of the Empire. In the pious Shi'ite tradition, this attitude of the legitimate Imams is given a religious colouring; their passivity was an expression of their devoutness and otherworldliness, their acquiescence an application of the principle of *Taqiyya*.

The term *Taqiyya*, caution, precaution, denotes an Islamic doctrine of dispensation – the idea that, under compulsion or menace, a believer may be dispensed from fulfilling certain obligations of religion. The principle is variously defined and interpreted, and is by no means peculiar to the Shi'a; it was they, however, who were most frequently exposed to the dangers of persecution and repression, and by them therefore that the principle was most frequently invoked. It was used to justify the concealment of beliefs likely to arouse the hostility of the authorities or the populace; it was cited as an answer to the self-destroying militancy that had led so many to their deaths in utterly hopeless rebellions.

The first half of the eighth century was a period of intensive activity among the extremist Shi'a. Countless sects and sub-sects appeared, especially among the mixed population of Southern

Iraq and the coasts of the Persian Gulf. Their doctrines were variable and eclectic, and transition was easy and frequent from one sect or leader to another. The Muslim sources name many religious preachers, some of them men of humble origin, who led revolts and were put to death, and attribute to some of them doctrines which were later characteristic of the Ismailis. One group practised strangling with cords as a religious duty – an obvious parallel to Indian Thuggee, and a foreshadowing of the 'assassinations' of later centuries. Even among those who were moderate in doctrine, there were militant groups who tried to seize power by force, and suffered defeat and destruction at the hands of the Umayyad and then of the Abbasid armies.

By the second half of the eighth century the early extremist and militant movements had, for the most part, failed, and had either disappeared or dwindled into insignificance. It was the legitimate Imams – moderate, pliant, yet resolute – who preserved and enriched the Shi'ite faith and prepared the way for a new and greater effort to win control of the world of Islam.

Despite these early failures, and despite the discouragement of the Imams themselves, extremist and militant elements continued to appear, even in the immediate entourage of the legitimate Imams. The decisive split between extremists and moderates occurred after the death in 765 of Ja'far al-Sadiq, the sixth Imam after Ali. Ja'far's eldest son was Isma'il. For reasons which are not quite clear, and probably because of his association with extremist elements, Isma'il was disinherited, and a large part of the Shi'a recognized his younger brother Musa al-Kazim as seventh Imam. The line of Musa continued until the twelfth Imam, who disappeared in about 873, and is still the 'awaited Imam' or Mahdi of the great majority of the Shi'a at the present day. The followers of the twelve Imams, known as the Ithna 'ashari or Twelver Shi'a, represent the more moderate branch of the sect. Their differences from the main body of Sunni Islam are limited to a certain number of points of doctrine, which in recent years have become ever less significant. Since the sixteenth century, Twelver Shi'ism has been the official religion of Iran.

Another group followed Isma'il and his descendants, and are

known as Ismailis (Ismā'īlīs). For long working in secret, they formed a sect which in cohesion and organization, in both intellectual and emotional appeal, far outstripped all its rivals. In place of the chaotic speculations and primitive superstitions of the earlier sects, a series of distinguished theologians elaborated a system of religious doctrine on a high philosophic level, and produced a literature which, after centuries of eclipse, is only now once again beginning to achieve recognition at its true worth. To the pious, the Ismailis offered respect for the Qur'an, for tradition and for law no less than that of the Sunnis. To the intellectual, they submitted a philosophical explanation of the universe, drawing on the sources of ancient and especially neoplatonic thought. To the spiritual, they brought a warm, personal, emotional faith, sustained by the example of the suffering of the Imams and the self-sacrifice of their followers – the experience of Passion, and the attainment of the Truth. To the discontented, finally, they offered the attraction of a well-organized, widespread and powerful opposition movement, which seemed to provide a real possibility of overthrowing the existing order, and establishing in its place a new and just society, headed by the Imam – the heir of the Prophet, the chosen of God, and the sole rightful leader of mankind.

The Imam is central to the Ismaili system — of doctrine and of organization, of loyalty and of action. After the creation of the world by the action of the universal mind on the universal soul, human history falls into a series of cycles, each begun by a 'speaking' imam, or prophet, followed by a succession of 'silent' imams. There were cycles of hidden and of manifest imams, corresponding to the periods of clandestinity and of success of the faith. The imams, in the current cycle the descendants of Ali and Fatima through Isma'il, were divinely inspired and infallible – in a sense indeed themselves divine, since the Imam was the microcosm, the personification of the metaphysical soul of the universe. As such, he was the fountainhead of knowledge and authority – of the esoteric truths that were hidden from the uninformed, and of commands that required total and unquestioning obedience.

For the initiate, there was the drama and excitement of secret knowledge and secret action. The former was made known through the *Taīwīl al-Bāṭin*, esoteric interpretation, a characteristic doctrine of the sect which gave rise to the term Batini, by which it was sometimes known. Besides their literal and obvious meaning, the prescriptions of the Qur'an and the traditions had a second meaning, an allegoric and esoteric interpretation which was revealed by the Imam and taught to the initiates. Some branches of the sect go even further, and adopt an antinomian doctrine that is recurrent in extremist Muslim heresy and mysticism. The ultimate religious obligation is knowledge – gnosis – of the true Imam; the literal meaning of the law is abrogated for the faithful, and survives, if at all, as a punishment for the profane. A common theme of Ismaili religious writings is the search for the Truth – at first vain, then culminating in a moment of blinding illumination. The organization and activities of the sect, and the custodianship and propagation of its teachings, were in the hands of a hierarchy of da'is, ranked under a chief da'i, who was the immediate helper of the Imam.

For the first century and a half after the death of Isma'il, the Ismaili Imams remained hidden, and little is known about the activities or even the teachings of the da'is. A new phase began in the second half of the ninth century, when the growing and manifest weakness of the Abbasid Caliphs in Baghdad seemed to portend the break-up of the Islamic Empire and the disruption of Islamic society. In the provinces, local dynasties appeared – usually military, sometimes tribal in origin; for the most part they were short-lived, and in some areas extortionate and oppressive. Even in the capital, the Caliphs were losing their power, and becoming helpless puppets in the hands of their own soldiery. The foundations of confidence and assent in the Islamic universal polity were crumbling, and men began to look elsewhere for comfort and reassurance. In these uncertain times, the message of the Shi'a – that the Islamic community had taken the wrong path, and must be brought back to the right one – was heard with new attention. Both branches of the Shi'a, the Twelvers and the Ismailis, profited from these opportunities, and at first it seemed as if the Twelvers were about to triumph. Twelver Shi'ite dynasties appeared in several places, and in 946 a Shi'ite dynasty from Persia, the Buyids, inflicted the ultimate humiliation on Sunni Islam by capturing Baghdad and bringing the Caliph himself under Shi'ite control. By this time, however, the Twelver Shi'ites had no Imam, for the twelfth and last had disappeared some seventy years previously. The Buyids, confronted with a crucial choice, decided not to recognize any other Alid claimant, but to retain the Abbasids as titular Caliphs, under their own domination and patronage. By so doing, they still further discredited the already tarnished Sunni Caliphate; at the same time, they finally eliminated moderate Shi'ism as a serious alternative to it.

There was much that made men seek an alternative. The great social and economic changes of the eighth and ninth centuries had brought wealth and power to some, hardship and frustration to others. In the countryside, the growth of large and, often, fiscally privileged estates was accompanied by the impoverishment and subjection of tenants and smallholders; in the towns, the development of commerce and industry created a class of journeyman labourers, and attracted an unstable and floating population of rootless and needy migrants. Amid great prosperity, there was also great distress. The dry legalism and remote transcendentalism of the orthodox faith, the cautious conformism of its accredited exponents, offered little comfort to the dispossessed, little scope for the spiritual yearnings of the uprooted and unhappy. There was an intellectual malaise, too. Muslim thought and learning, enriched from many sources, were becoming more subtle, more sophisticated, more diverse. There were great and agonizing problems to be considered, arising from the confrontation of Islamic revelation, Greek science and philosophy, Persian wisdom, and the hard facts of history. Among many, there was a loss of confidence in traditional Islamic answers, and a desire, of growing urgency, for new ones. The great Islamic consensus – religious, philosophical, political, social – seemed to be breaking up; a new principle of unity and authority, just and effective, was needed to save Islam from destruction.

It was the great strength of the Ismailis that they could offer such a principle – a design for a new world order under the Imam. To both the devout and the discontented, the message and ministrations of the da'is brought comfort and promise. To philosophers and theologians, poets and scholars, the Ismaili synthesis offered a seductive appeal. Because of the strong reactions against the Ismailis in later times, most of their literature disappeared from the central lands of Islam, and was preserved only among the sectaries themselves. But a few works of Ismaili inspiration have for long been widely known, and many of the great classical authors in Arabic and Persian show at least traces of Ismaili influence. The 'Epistles of the Sincere Brethren', a famous encyclopaedia of religious and worldly knowledge compiled in the tenth century, is saturated with Ismaili thought, and exercised a profound influence on Muslim intellectual life from Persia to Spain.

Not surprisingly, the da'is achieved special success in those places, like Southern Iraq, the shores of the Persian Gulf, and parts of Persia, where earlier forms of militant and extremist Shi'ism had already won a following, or where local cults offered favourable ground. At the end of the ninth century a branch of the sect known as the Carmathians – their precise relationship with the main Ismaili body is uncertain – was able to win control and establish a form of republic in Eastern Arabia, which served them for more than a century as a base for military and propagandist operations against the Caliphate. A Carmathian attempt to seize power in Syria at the beginning of the tenth century failed, but the episode is significant and reveals some local support for Ismailism even at that early date.

The greatest triumph of the Ismaili cause came in another quarter. A mission to the Yemen had, by the end of the ninth century, won many converts and a base of political power; from there further missions were despatched to other countries, including India and North Africa, where they achieved their most spectacular success. By 909 they were strong enough for the hidden Imam to emerge from hiding and proclaim himself Caliph in North Africa, with the title al-Mahdi, thus founding a new state and dynasty. They were known as the Fatimids, in token of their descent from Fatima, the daughter of the Prophet.

In the first half-century, the Fatimid Caliphs ruled in the west only, in North Africa and Sicily. Their eyes, however, were on the East, the heartlands of Islam, where alone they could hope to achieve their purpose of ousting the Sunni Abbasid Caliphs and establishing themselves as sole heads of all Islam. Ismaili agents and missionaries were active in all the Sunni lands; Fatimid armies prepared in Tunisia for the conquest of Egypt – the first step on the road to the Empire of the East.

In 969 this first step was duly completed. Fatimid troops conquered the Nile valley, and were soon advancing across Sinai into Palestine and Southern Syria. Near Fustat, the old seat of government, the Fatimid leaders built a new city, called Cairo, as the capital of their Empire, and a new mosque-university, called al-Azhar, as the citadel of their faith. The Caliph, al-Mu'izz, moved from Tunisia to his new residence, where his descendants reigned for the next two hundred years.

The Ismaili challenge to the old order was now closer and stronger, and was maintained by a great power – for a while the greatest in the Islamic world. The Fatimid Empire at its peak included Egypt, Syria, North Africa, Sicily, the Red Sea coast of Africa, the Yemen and the Hijaz in Arabia, with the holy cities of Mecca and Medina. In addition the Fatimid Caliph controlled a vast network of da'is and commanded the allegiance of count-less followers in the lands still subject to the Sunni rulers of the East. In the great colleges of Cairo, scholars and teachers elabor-ated the doctrines of the Ismaili faith and trained missionaries to preach them to the unconverted at home and abroad. One of their main areas of activity was Persia and Central Asia, from which many aspirers after the truth found their way to Cairo, and to which in due course they returned as skilled exponents of the Ismaili message. Outstanding among them was the philosopher and poet Nasir-i Khusraw. Converted during a visit to Egypt in 1046, he returned to preach Ismailism in the eastern lands, where he exercised a powerful influence.

The Sunni response was at first limited and ineffectual – security measures against the da'is, and political warfare against the Fatimids, who in a manifesto published in Baghdad in 1011 were accused, somewhat unconvincingly, of not being Fatimids at all, but descendants of a disreputable impostor.

Yet, despite this imposing strength, and a great effort of political, religious and economic warfare against the Abbasid Caliphate, the Fatimid challenge failed. The Abbasid Caliphate survived; Sunni Islam recovered and triumphed – and the Fatimid Caliphs successively lost their Empire, their authority and their following.

Part of the reason for this failure must be sought in events in the East, where great changes were taking place. The coming of the Turkish peoples interrupted the political fragmentation of South West Asia, and for a while restored to the lands of the Sunni Caliphate the unity and stability which they had lost. The Turkish conquerors were new converts, earnest, loyal, and orthodox; they were imbued with a strong sense of their duty to Islam, and of their responsibility, as the new protectors of the Caliph and masters of the Muslim world, to sustain and defend it against internal and external dangers. This duty they discharged to the full. Turkish rulers and Turkish soldiers provided the political and military strength and skill to withstand, contain, and repel the two great dangers that threatened Sunni Islam – the challenge of the Ismaili Caliphs and, later, the invasion of the Crusaders from Europe.

The same dangers – of religious schism and foreign invasion – helped to stimulate the great Sunni revival which was beginning to gather force. In the Sunni world there were still great reserves of religious power – in the theology of the schoolmen, the spirituality of the mystics, and the pious devotion of their followers. In this time of crisis and recovery a new synthesis was achieved, with an answer both to the intellectual challenge of Ismaili thought and to the emotional appeal of Ismaili faith.

While their Sunni adversaries were gaining in political, military and religious strength, the Ismaili Fatimid cause was weakened by religious dissension and political decline. The first serious internal conflicts in Ismailism resulted from the very successes of the Fatimids. The needs and responsibilities of a dynasty and an empire required some modification in earlier doctrines, and, in the words of a modern Ismaili scholar, the adoption of 'a graver and more conservative attitude towards the then existing institution of Islam'.[1] From the first, there were disputes between Ismaili radicals and conservatives, between the preservers and the revealers of the esoteric mysteries. From time to time the Fatimid Caliphs had to face schism, and even armed opposition, as groups of their followers withdrew their assent and support. Already in the time of the first Fatimid Caliph in North Africa, there were controversies between da'is of different views, and some defections from the Fatimid camp. The fourth Caliph, al-Mu'izz, faced similar difficulties; at the very moment of his triumph, during the conquest of Egypt, he even had to fight against the Carmathians from Eastern Arabia who, after first supporting the Fatimids, turned against them and attacked their armies in Syria and Egypt. At a later date the Carmathians seem to have returned to the Fatimid allegiance, and disappeared as a separate entity. Another schism occurred after the disappearance, in obscure circumstances, of the sixth Caliph al-Hakim in 1021. A group of the faithful believed that al-Hakim was divine, and had not died but gone into occultation. Refusing to recognize his successors on the Fatimid throne, they seceded from the main body of the sect. They had some success in winning support among the Ismailis of Syria, where groups of them still survive, in the present-day states of Syria, Lebanon and Israel. One of the founders of this sect was a da'i of Central Asian origin called Muhammad ibn Isma'il al-Darazi. They are still known, after him, as Druzes.

During the long reign of the eighth Caliph al-Mustansir (1036–94) the Fatimid Empire reached its peak and fell into a swift decline; at his death the Ismaili mission was torn apart by its greatest internal schism.

In the prime of Fatimid power the Caliph retained full personal control of affairs, presiding with equal authority over the three great branches of government – the bureaucracy, the religious hierarchy, and the armed forces. The head of the civil bureaucracy, and the effective head of the government under the Caliph, was the vizier, a civilian; the head of the religious hierarchy was the chief of the da'is or missionaries (*dā'ī al-du'āt*), who besides controlling the Ismaili establishment within the Empire also commanded the great army of Ismaili agents and missionaries abroad. The commander of the armed forces, in what was essentially a civilian régime, headed the third branch. Since the death of al-Hakim, however, the military had been steadily increasing their power at the expense of the civilians and even of the Caliph himself. The setbacks, misfortunes, and upheavals of the mid-eleventh century accelerated this process; it was completed in 1074 when, at the Caliph's invitation, Badr al-Jamali, the military governor of Acre, moved into Egypt with his own army to take control of affairs. He was soon master of the country, with the three titles, conferred by the Caliph, of Commander of the Armies, Chief of the Missionaries, and vizier – signifying his control over all three branches, the military, religious, and bureaucratic. It is by the first of these titles that he was usually known.

Henceforth the real master of Egypt was the Commander of the Armies, a military autocrat ruling through his troops. The post became a permanency, in which Badr al-Jamali was succeeded by his son and grandson, and then by a series of other military autocrats. Just as the Abbasid Caliphs in Baghdad had become the helpless puppets of their own praetorians, so now the Fatimids became mere figureheads for a succession of military dictators. It was a sad decline for a dynasty which had claimed the spiritual and political headship of all Islam – a decline that was in striking contradiction with the beliefs and hopes of the Ismaili faith.

Such a change inevitably awoke discontent and opposition among the more militant and consistent of the sectaries, the more so since it coincided with a period of renewed activity among the Ismailis in Persia. The replacement of Badr al-Jamali by his son al-Afdal in 1094 made little change in the state of affairs, and when, on the death of al-Mustansir a few months later, the Commander of the Armies was confronted with the need to choose a new Caliph, his choice was not difficult. On the one hand there was Nizar, the eldest son and an adult, already appointed heir by al-Mustansir, known and accepted by the Ismaili leaders; on the other his younger brother al-Musta'li, a youth without allies or supporters, who would consequently be entirely dependent on his powerful patron. It was no doubt with this in mind that al-Afdal arranged a marriage between his own daughter and al-Musta'li and, on al-Mustansir's death, proclaimed his son-in-law as Caliph. Nizar fled to Alexandria, where he rose in revolt with local support. After some initial success, he was defeated, captured, and later killed.

In choosing al-Musta'li, al-Afdal split the sect from top to bottom, and alienated, perhaps intentionally, almost the whole of its following in the eastern lands of Islam. Even within the Fatimid boundaries there were movements of opposition; the Eastern Ismailis refused to recognize the new Caliph and, proclaiming their allegiance to Nizar and his line, broke off all relations with the attenuated Fatimid organization in Cairo. The divergence between the state and the revolutionaries, which had begun to appear when the state was first established, was now complete.

Before long, even those Ismailis who had accepted al-Musta'li broke their links with the régime in Cairo. In 1130, after the murder of al-Amir, the son and successor of al-Musta'li, by supporters of the Nizaris, the remaining Ismailis refused to recognize the new Caliph in Cairo, and adopted the belief that a lost, infant son of al-Amir, called Tayyib, was the hidden and awaited Imam. There were to be no more Imams after him.

Four more Fatimid Caliphs reigned in Cairo, but they were no more than a local Egyptian dynasty, without power, influence or hope. In 1171, as the last of them lay dying in his palace, the Kurdish soldier Saladin, who had meanwhile become the real master of Egypt, allowed a preacher to recite the bidding-prayer in the name of the Abbasid Caliph of Baghdad. The Fatimid Caliphate, already dead both as a religious and as a political force, was now formally abolished, amid the almost total indifference of the population. The heretical books of the Ismailis were heaped on bonfires. After more than two centuries, Egypt was restored to the Sunni fold.

By this time, there can have been few convinced Ismailis left in Egypt. In other lands, however, the sect survived, in the two main branches into which it had divided on the death of al-Mustansir. The followers of al-Musta'li were – and still are – to be found mainly in the Yemen and in India, where they are known as Bohras. Their form of Ismailism is sometimes called the 'old preaching' since it carried on the main doctrinal traditions of the Fatimid period.

While the Musta'lians stagnated in the remoter outposts of Islam, their rivals the Nizaris, the supporters of Nizar, entered on a period of intensive development, both in doctrine and in political action, and for a while played an important and dramatic role in the affairs of Islam.

In the eleventh century the growing internal weakness of the Islamic world was revealed by a series of invasions, the most important of which, that of the Seljuq Turks, created a new military Empire stretching from Central Asia to the Mediterranean. Associated with these invasions were important economic, social and cultural changes, of profound importance in the history of Islam. In the customary aftermath of conquest, vast lands and revenues were assigned to the officers of the victorious Turkish armies, who, with their officials, formed a new ruling element, displacing or overshadowing the Arab and Persian aristocracy and gentry of earlier times. Power, wealth and status belonged to new men – alien newcomers who, often, were still imperfectly assimilated to the urban civilization of the Islamic Middle East. The position of the old elite was further weakened by other factors – the movement of nomads, the shift of trade-routes, the beginnings of the great changes that led to the rise of Europe and the relative decline of Islam. In a time of trouble and danger, the new Turkish masters brought a measure of strength and order – but at a cost of higher military expenditure, firmer control of public life, and stricter conformity of thought.

The military power of the Turks was unshakable – the orthodoxy of the schools was no longer open to serious challenge. But there were other methods of attack, and to the many malcontents of the Seljuq Empire Ismailism, in its new form, once again brought a seductive critique of orthodoxy, now associated with a new and effective strategy of revolt. The 'old preaching' of Ismailism had failed; the Fatimid Empire was dying. A 'new preaching' and a new method were needed. They were devised by a revolutionary of genius, called Hasan-i Sabbah.

3

The New Preaching

Hasan-i Sabbah was born in the city of Qumm, one of the first centres of Arab settlement in Persia and a stronghold of Twelver Shi'ism.¹ His father, a Twelver Shi'ite, had come from Kufa in Iraq, and was said to be of Yemeni origin – more fancifully, a descendant of the ancient Himyaritic kings of Southern Arabia. The date of Hasan's birth is unknown, but was probably about the middle of the eleventh century. When he was still a child, his father moved to Rayy – by the modern city of Tehran – and it was there that Hasan pursued his religious education. Rayy had been a centre of activity of the da'is since the ninth century, and it was not long before Hasan began to feel their influence. In an autobiographical fragment, preserved by later historians, he tells his own story:

'From the days of my boyhood, from the age of seven, I felt a love for the various branches of learning, and wished to become a religious scholar; until the age of seventeen I was a seeker and searcher for knowledge, but kept to the Twelver faith of my fathers.

'In Rayy I met a man, one of the Comrades [*Rafiq*, a term often used by the Ismailis of themselves] called Amira Zarrab, who from time to time expounded the doctrine of the Caliphs of Egypt ... as Nasir-i Khusraw had done before him ...

'There had never been any doubt or uncertainty in my faith in Islam; in my belief that there is a living, enduring, all-powerful, all-hearing, all-seeing God, a Prophet and an Imam, permitted things and forbidden things, heaven and hell, commandment and forbidding. I supposed that religion and doctrine consisted of that which people in general, and the Shi'a in particular, possessed, and it never entered my mind that truth should be sought outside Islam. I thought that the doctrines of the Ismailis were philosophy [a term of abuse among the pious], and the ruler of Egypt a philosophizer.

'Amira Zarrab was a man of good character. When he first conversed with me, he said: "The Ismailis say such and such." I said: "O friend, do not speak their words, for they are outcasts, and what they say is against religion." There were controversies and debates between us, and he disproved and destroyed my belief. I did not admit this to him, but in my heart these words had great effect ... Amira said to me: "When you think in your bed at night you know that what I say convinces you".'

Later Hasan and his mentor were separated, but the young disciple continued his search, and read Ismaili books, where he found some things that convinced him, and others that left him dissatisfied. A severe and terrible illness completed his conversion. 'I thought: surely this is the true faith, and because of my great fear I did not acknowledge it. Now my appointed time has come, and I shall die without having attained the truth.'

Hasan did not die, and on his recovery he sought out another Ismaili teacher, who completed his instruction. His next step was to take the oath of allegiance to the Fatimid Imam; it was administered to him by a missionary who held his licence from Abd al-Malik Ibn Attash, the chief of the Ismaili *da'wa*, or mission, in Western Persia and Iraq. Shortly after, in May–June 1072, the chief in person visited Rayy, where he met the new recruit. He approved of him, gave him an appointment in the *da'wa*, and told him to go to Cairo and present himself at the Caliph's court – in other words, to report to headquarters.[2]

It was not in fact until several years later that Hasan went to Egypt. A story related by several Persian authors, and introduced to European readers by Edward Fitzgerald in the preface to his translation of the *Rubaiyat*, purports to give an account of the events leading to his departure. According to this tale, Hasan-i Sabbah, the poet Omar Khayyam, and the vizier Nizam al-Mulk, had all been fellow-students of the same teacher. The three made a

pact that whichever of them first achieved success and fortune in
the world would help the other two. Nizam al-Mulk in due course
became the vizier of the Sultan, and his schoolmates put forward
their claims. Both were offered governorships, which they both
refused, though for very different reasons. Omar Khayyam
shunned the responsibilities of office, and preferred a pension
and the enjoyment of leisure; Hasan refused to be fobbed off with
a provincial post, and sought high office at court. Given his wish,
he soon became a candidate for the vizierate and a dangerous
rival to Nizam al-Mulk himself. The vizier therefore plotted
against him, and by a trick managed to disgrace him in the eyes
of the Sultan. Shamed and resentful, Hasan-i Sabbah fled to Egypt,
where he prepared his revenge.

The story presents some difficulties. Nizam al-Mulk was born
at the latest in 1020, and was killed in 1092. The dates of birth
of Hasan-i Sabbah and Omar Khayyam are unknown, but the
former died in 1124, the latter at the earliest in 1123. The dates
make it very unlikely that all three could have been contemporaries
as students, and most modern scholars have rejected this
picturesque tale as a fable.[3] A more credible explanation of
Hasan's departure is given by other historians; according to this
version, he fell foul of the authorities in Rayy, who accused him of
harbouring Egyptian agents and of being a dangerous agitator.
To escape arrest he fled from the city, and embarked on the series
of journeys which were to bring him to Egypt.[4]

According to the autobiographical fragment, he left Rayy in
1076 and went to Isfahan. From there he travelled northward
to Azerbayjan, and thence to Mayyafariqin, where he was driven
out of town by the Qadi for asserting the exclusive right of the
Imam to interpret religion, and thus denying the authority of the
Sunni Ulema. Continuing through Mesopotamia and Syria, he
reached Damascus, where he found that the overland route to
Egypt was blocked by military disturbances. He therefore turned
west to the coast, and, travelling southwards from Beirut, sailed
from Palestine to Egypt. He arrived in Cairo on 30 August 1078,
and was greeted by high dignitaries of the Fatimid court.

Hasan-i Sabbah stayed in Egypt for about three years, first in

Cairo and then in Alexandria. According to some accounts, he came into conflict with the Commander of the Armies Badr al-Jamali because of his support for Nizar, and was imprisoned and then deported from the country. The reason given for the conflict must be a later embellishment, since the dispute over the succession had not yet arisen at the time, but a collision between the ardent revolutionary and the military dictator is far from unlikely.[5]

From Egypt he was deported to North Africa, but the Frankish ship on which he was travelling was wrecked, and he was saved and taken to Syria. Travelling through Aleppo and Baghdad, he reached Isfahan on 10 June 1081. For the next nine years he travelled extensively in Persia, in the service of the *da'wa*. In the autobiographical fragment he speaks of several such journeys: 'From thence [i.e. from Isfahan] I proceeded to Kerman and Yazd, and conducted propaganda there for a while.'[6] From central Iran he returned to Isfahan, and then turned south to spend three months in Khuzistan, where he had already spent some time while on his way back from Egypt.

To an increasing extent he began to concentrate his attention on the far north of Persia – on the Caspian provinces of Gilan and Mazandaran, and especially on the highland region known as Daylam. These lands, lying north of the mountain chain that bounds the great plateau of Iran, are markedly different in geographical configuration from the rest of the country, and were inhabited by a hardy, warlike and independent people, for long regarded by the Iranians of the plateau as alien and dangerous. In ancient times, the rulers of Iran had never been able to effectively to subjugate them, and even the Sasanids had found it necessary to maintain border fortresses as defensive bastions against their incursions. The Arab conquerors of Iran fared little better. It is said that when the Arab leader al-Hajjaj was about to attack Daylam, he had a map of the country prepared, depicting the mountains, valleys and passes; he showed it to a Daylami delegation, and called upon them to surrender before he invaded and devastated their country. They looked at the map, and said: 'They have informed you correctly concerning our country, and this is its picture – except that they have not shown the warriors who defend these passes and mountains. You will learn about them if you try.'7 In time, Daylam was Islamized – by peaceful penetration rather than by conquest.

Among the last to submit to Islam, the Daylamis were among the first to reassert their individuality within it – politically, by the emergence of independent dynasties, religiously, through the adoption of unorthodox beliefs. From the end of the eighth century, when members of the house of Ali, fleeing from Abbasid persecution, found refuge and support there, Daylam became a centre of Shi'ite activity, jealously guarding its independence against the Caliphs of Baghdad and other Sunni rulers. During the tenth century, under the Buyids, the Daylamis even succeeded in establishing their ascendancy over most of Persia and Iraq, and were for a while the custodians of the Caliphs themselves. The coming of the Seljuqs put an end to Daylami and Shi'ite rule in the Empire, and pressed hard on Daylam itself.

It was among these northern peoples – predominantly Shi'ite and already strongly infiltrated by Ismaili propaganda – that Hasan-i Sabbah made his main effort. For the warlike and disaffected inhabitants of the mountains of Daylam and Mazarandan, his militant creed had a powerful appeal. Avoiding the cities, he made his way through the deserts from Khuzistan to eastern Mazandaran, and eventually established himself in Damghan, where he stayed for three years. From this base he despatched da'is to work among the mountain-dwellers, and himself travelled tirelessly to direct and assist their efforts. His activities soon attracted the attention of the vizier, who ordered the authorities in Rayy to capture him. They did not succeed. Avoiding Rayy, he travelled by the mountain route to Qazvin, the most convenient base for a campaign in Daylam.

During his interminable journeys, Hasan was not only occupied with winning converts to the cause. He was also concerned with finding a new kind of base – not a clandestine tryst in a city, in constant danger of discovery and disruption, but a remote and inaccessible stronghold, from which he could with impunity direct his war against the Seljuq Empire. His choice finally fell on the castle of Alamut, built on a narrow ridge on the top of a high rock in the heart of the Elburz mountains, and dominating an enclosed and cultivated valley, about thirty miles long and three miles wide at the broadest point. More than 6,000 feet above sea-level, the castle was several hundred feet above the base of the rock, and could be reached only by a narrow, steep and winding path. The approach to the rock was through the narrow gorge of the Alamut river, between perpendicular and sometimes overhanging cliffs.

The castle is said to have been built by one of the kings of Daylam. While out hunting one day, he loosed a manned eagle, which alighted on the rock. The king saw the strategic value of the site, and at once built a castle upon it. 'And he called it Aluh Amut, which in the Daylami language means the eagle's teaching.'[8] Others, less convincingly, translate the name as the eagle's nest. The castle was rebuilt by an Alid ruler in 860, and at the time of Hasan's arrival was in the hands of an Alid called Mihdi, who held it from the Seljuq Sultan.

The seizure of Alamut was carefully prepared. From Damghan, Hasan had sent da'is to work in the villages around Alamut. Then 'from Qazvin I again sent a da'i to the castle of Alamut ... Some of the people in Alamut were converted by the da'i and they sought to convert the Alid also. He pretended to be won over but afterwards contrived to send down all the converts and then closed the gates of the castle saying that it belonged to the Sultan. After much discussion he readmitted them and after that they refused to go down at his bidding.'[9]

With his followers now installed in the castle, Hasan left Qazvin for the neighbourhood of Alamut, where he stayed for some time in concealment. Then, on Wednesday, 4 September 1090, he was brought secretly into the castle. For a while he remained in the castle in disguise, but in due course his identity became known. The former owner realized what had happened, but could do nothing to stop or change it. Hasan allowed him to leave, and, according to a story related by the Persian chroniclers, gave him a draft for 3,000 gold dinars, in payment for his castle.[10]

Hasan-i Sabbah was now firmly established as master of

Alamut. From the time of his entry until his death thirty five years later, he never once went down from the rock, and only twice left the house in which he lived. On both occasions he went up on the roof. 'The rest of the time until his death,' says Rashid al-Din, 'he passed inside the house where he lived; he was occupied with reading books, committing the words of the *da'wa* to writing, and administering the affairs of his realm, and he lived an ascetic, abstemious, and pious life.'[11]

At first, his task was twofold – to win converts, and to gain possession of more castles. From Alamut he sent missionaries and agents in various directions, to accomplish both purposes. An obvious objective was control of the immediate neighbourhood of his headquarters, the district called Rudbar, river-bed, after the river Shah Rud which flows through it. In these remote but fertile mountain valleys, an older way of life persisted, unaffected by the changes that had been taking place further south. There was no real town in Rudbar, and no town-based military or political authority. The people lived in villages, and gave their allegiance to a local gentry who lived in castles. It was among these, as well as among the villagers, that the Ismailis found support. 'Hasan exerted every effort,' says Juvayni, 'to capture the places adjacent to Alamut or that vicinity. Where possible he won them over by the tricks of his propaganda while such places as were unaffected by his blandishments he seized with slaughter, ravishment, pillage, bloodshed, and war. He took such castles as he could and wherever he found a suitable rock he built a castle upon it.'[12] An important success was the capture by assault of the castle of Lamasar in 1096 or 1102.[13] The attackers were led by Kiya Burzurgumid, who remained there as commandant for twenty years. Strategically situated on a rounded rock overlooking the Shah Rud, this castle confirmed the power of the Ismailis in the whole Rudbar area.

Far away to the south-east lay the barren, mountainous country of Quhistan, near the present border between Persia and Afghanistan. Its population lived in a scattered and isolated group of oases surrounded on all sides by the great salt desert of the central plateau. In early Islamic times, this region had been one of the last refuges of Zoroastrianism; converted to Islam, it became a resort of Shi'ite and other religious dissidents and, later, of the Ismailis. In 1091–2 Hasan-i Sabbah sent a missionary to Quhistan, to mobilize and extend Ismaili support. His choice fell on Husayn Qa'ini, an able da'i who had played some role in the conversion of Alamut, and who was himself of Quhistani origin. His mission was immediately successful. The population of Quhistan were chafing under Seljuq rule; an oppressive Seljuq officer, it is said, brought matters to a head by demanding the sister of the highly respected local lord, who thereupon defected to the Ismailis. What happened in Quhistan was more than secret subversion, more than the seizure of castles; it assumed almost the character of a popular rising, a movement for independence from alien, military domination. In many parts of the province the Ismailis rose in open revolt, and seized control of several of the main towns – Zuzan, Qa'in, Tabas, Tun, and others. In eastern Quhistan, as in Rudbar, they succeeded in creating what was virtually a territorial state.[14]

Mountainous areas had obvious advantages for the Ismaili strategy of expansion. Another such area lay in South Western Persia, in the region between Khuzistan and Fars. There too there were the necessary conditions for success – difficult country, a turbulent and disaffected population, a strong local tradition of Shi'ite and Ismaili loyalties. The Ismaili leader in this area was Abu Hamza, a shoemaker from Arrajan who had been to Egypt and returned as a Fatimid da'i. He seized two castles, a few miles from Arrajan, and used them as a base for further activity.[15]

While some Ismaili missionaries were acquiring and consolidating positions of strength in remote outposts, others were carrying their religious propaganda into the main centres of Sunni orthodoxy and Seljuq power. It was they who brought about the first bloodshed involving Ismaili agents and the Seljuq authorities. The first incident occurred in a small town called Sava, in the northern plateau not far from Rayy and Qumm, perhaps even before the capture of Alamut. A group of eighteen Ismailis was arrested by the police-chief for joining together in separate prayers. This was their first such meeting, and after questioning they were allowed to go free. They then tried to convert a muezzin from Sava who was living in Isfahan. He refused to respond to their appeal and the Ismailis, fearing that he would denounce them, murdered him. He, says the Arabic historian Ibn al-Athir, was their first victim, and his was the first blood that they shed. News of this murder reached the vizier, Nizam al-Mulk, who personally gave orders for the execution of the ringleader. The man accused was a carpenter called Tahir, the son of a preacher who had held various religious offices, and had been lynched by a mob in Kerman as a suspected Ismaili. Tahir was executed and made an example of, and his body dragged through the market-place. He, says Ibn al-Athir, was the first Ismaili to be executed.[16]

In 1092 the Seljuqs made their first effort to deal with the Ismaili menace by military force. Malikshah, the Great Sultan, or supreme overlord of the Seljuq rulers and princes, sent two expeditions, one against Alamut, the other against Quhistan. Both were repelled, the former with the help of supporters and sympathizers from Rudbar and from Qazvin itself. Juvayni cites an Ismaili account of the victory: 'Sultan Malikshah, in the beginning of the year 485/1092, dispatched an emir called Arslantash to expel and extirpate Hasan-i Sabbah and all his followers. This emir sat down before Alamut in Jumada I of the said year [June–July, 1092]. At that time Hasan-i Sabbah had with him on Alamut no more than 60 or 70 men; and they had but few stores. They lived on the little they had, a bare subsistence, and kept up the battle with the besiegers. Now one of Hasan's da'is, a man called Dihdar Bu-Ali, who came from Zuvara and Ardistan, had his residence in Qazvin, some of the inhabitants of which were his converts; as likewise in the district of Talaqan and Kuh-i Bara and the district of Rayy many people believed in the Sabbahian propaganda; and they all resorted to the man who had settled in Qazvin. Hasan-i Sabbah now appealed to Bu-Ali for help, and he stirred up a host of people from Kuh-i Bara and Talaqan and likewise sent arms and implements of war from Qazvin. Some 300 of these men came to the aid of Hasan-i Sabbah. They threw themselves into Alamut and then with the assistance of the garrison and the support of some of the people of Rudbar, who were in league with them outside the castle, one night at the end of Sha'ban of that year [September–October, 1092], they made a surprise attack upon the army of Arslantash. By divine pre-ordination the army was put to flight and leaving Alamut returned to Malikshah.'¹⁷ The siege of the Ismaili centre in Quhistan was raised when news was received of the death of the Sultan in November 1092.

Meanwhile the Ismailis had achieved their first great success in the art that was to take its name from them – the art of assassination. Their chosen victim was the all-powerful vizier himself, whose efforts to 'stem the pus of sedition and excise the virus of inaction' had made him their most dangerous enemy. Hasan-i Sabbah laid his plans carefully: 'Our Master', says Rashid al-Din, following – and no doubt adjusting – his Ismaili source, 'laid snares and traps so as to catch first of all such fine game as Nizam al-Mulk in the net of death and perdition, and by this act his fame and renown became great. With the jugglery of deceit and the trickery of untruth, with guileful preparations and specious obfuscations, he laid the foundations of the fida'is, and he said: "who of you will rid this state of the evil of Nizam al-Mulk Tusi?" A man called Bu Tahir Arrani laid the hand of acceptance on his breast, and, following the path of error by which he hoped to attain the bliss of the world-to-come, on the night of Friday, the 12th of Ramadan of the year 485 [16 October 1092], in the district of Nihavand at the stage of Sahna, he came in the guise of a Sufi to the litter of Nizam al-Mulk, who was being borne from the audience-place to the tent of his women, and struck him with a knife, and by that blow he suffered martyrdom. Nizam al-Mulk was the first man whom the fida'is killed. Our Master, upon him what he deserves, said: "The killing of this devil is the beginning of bliss."'¹⁸

It was the first of a long series of such attacks which, in a calculated war of terror, brought sudden death to sovereigns, princes, generals, governors, and even divines who had condemned Ismaili doctrines and authorized the suppression of those who professed them. 'To kill them,' said one such pious opponent, 'is more lawful than rainwater. It is the duty of Sultans and kings to conquer and kill them, and cleanse the surface of the earth from their pollution. It is not right to associate or form friendships with them, nor to eat meat butchered by them, nor to enter into marriage with them. To shed the blood of a heretic is more meritorious than to kill seventy Greek infidels.'[19]

For their victims, the assassins were criminal fanatics, engaged in a murderous conspiracy against religion and society. For the Ismailis, they were a corps d'élite in the war against the enemies of the Imam; by striking down oppressors and usurpers, they gave the ultimate proof of their faith and loyalty, and earned immediate and eternal bliss. The Ismailis themselves used the term *fidā'i*, roughly devotee, of the actual murderer, and an interesting Ismaili poem has been preserved praising their courage, loyalty, and self-less devotion.[20] In the local Ismaili chronicles of Alamut, cited by Rashid al-Din and Kashani, there is a roll of honour of assassinations, giving the names of the victims and of their pious executioners.

In form, the Ismailis were a secret society, with a system of oaths and initiations and a graded hierarchy of rank and know-ledge. The secrets were well kept, and information about them is fragmentary and confused. Orthodox polemists depict the Ismailis as a band of deceitful nihilists who misled their dupes through successive stages of degradation, in the last of which they revealed the full horror of their unbelief. Ismaili writers see the sect as custodians of sacred mysteries, to which the believer could attain only after a long course of preparation and instruction, marked by progressive initiations. The term most commonly used for the organization of the sect is *da'wa* (in Persian *da'vat*), meaning mission or preaching; its agents are the da'is, or mis-sionaries – literally summoners, who constitute something like an ordained priesthood. In later Ismaili accounts they are variously divided into higher and lower ranks of preachers, teachers, and licentiates. Below them come the *mustajibs*, literally respondents, the lowest rank of initiates; above them is the *hujja* (Persian *hujjat*), or Proof, the senior da'i. The word *jazira*, island, is used to desi nate the territorial or ethnic jurisdiction over which a da'i presides. Like other Islamic sects and orders, the Ismailis often refer to their religious leaders as Elder – Arabic *Shaykh* or Persian *Pir*. A term commonly used for members of the sect is *rafiq* – comrade.[21]

In 1094 the Ismailis faced a major crisis. The Fatimid Caliph al-Mustansir, Imam of the time and head of the faith, died in Cairo, leaving a disputed succession. The Ismailis in Persia refused to recognize his successor on the Egyptian throne, and declared their belief that the rightful heir was his ousted elder son Nizar (see above, pp. 34–5). Until this split, the organization in Persia, at least nominally, had been under the supreme authority of the Imam and the Chief Da'i in Cairo. Hasan-i Sabbah had been their agent, first as deputy, then as successor of Abd al-Malik ibn Attash. There was now a complete break, and henceforth the Persian Ismailis neither enjoyed the support nor endured the control of their former masters in Cairo.

A crucial problem was the identity of the Imam – the central figure in the whole theological and political system of the Ismailis. Nizar had been the rightful Imam after al-Mustansir – but Nizar was murdered in prison in Alexandria, and his sons were said to have been killed with him. Some of the Nizaris claimed that Nizar was not really dead but in concealment and would return as Mahdi – that is to say, that the line of Imams was at an end. This school did not survive. What Hassan-i Sabbah taught his followers on this point is not known, but later the doctrine was adopted that the Imamate passed to a grandson of Nizar, who was secretly brought up in Alamut. In one version it was an infant that was smuggled from Egypt to Persia; in another it was a pregnant concubine of Nizar's son that was taken to Alamut, where she gave birth to the new Imam. According to Nizari belief, these things were kept strictly secret at the time, and not made known until many years later.

The absence of a manifest Imam, and the adjustments made necessary by the rupture with Cairo, do not seem to have halted or impeded the activities of the Ismailis in Persia. On the contrary, taking advantage of the temporary disarray of the Seljuq state during the last years of the eleventh and the first years of the twelfth century, they extended their activities to new areas.

One of these actions, the seizure of a castle in the eastern Elburz in 1096, was along the lines of their earlier efforts. Emissaries were sent from Alamut to the region of Damghan, where Hasan had worked before going to Daylam. They were greatly helped by the governor of Damghan, an officer called Muzaffar, a secret convert to Ismailism who had been won over by no less a person than Abd al-Malik ibn Attāsh. South of Damghan lay the fortress of Girdkuh, well suited by its strength and position to the purposes of the sect, and Muzaffar set to work to get it for them. Still posing as a loyal officer, he persuaded the Seljuq emir who was his superior to request Girdkuh from the Sultan, and to install him there as commandant. The emir and the Sultan both agreed, and Muzaffar duly took possession of Girdkuh. With the authority and probably at the expense of the emir, he repaired and fortified the castle, and stocked it with stores and treasure. Then, when his preparations were complete, he declared himself an Ismaili and a follower of Hasan-i Sabbah. He ruled it for 40 years. The castle of Girdkuh, overlooking the main route between Khurasan and Western Iran, and conveniently near to the centres of Ismaili support in eastern Mazandaran, greatly strengthened the strategic position of the growing Ismaili power.[22]

At about the same time they brought off a far bolder coup – the capture of the fortress called Shahdiz on a hill by the great city of Isfahan, the seat of a Seljuq Sultan.[23] Ismaili emissaries had been at work in this city for a long time; Abd al-Malik ibn Attāsh had lived there, but had fled when he was accused of Shi'ism. The struggles of the new Sultan Berkyaruq against his half-brothers and stepmother gave them a new chance, and they established a reign of terror in Isfahan which ended only when the populace rose against them and massacred them. Similar outbreaks of mob violence against the Ismailis are recorded in other Persian cities.

A new start was made in Isfahan by Ahmad, the son of Abd al-Malik ibn Attāsh. At the time of his father's flight he had been allowed to stay, since he was believed not to share his father's religious opinions. He was however secretly working for the Ismaili cause. A Persian historian says that he found a post as schoolteacher for the children of the garrison of Shahdiz which consisted, significantly, of Daylami mercenaries. By this means he ingratiated himself with them, and won them over to Ismailism. Thus he was able to gain possession of the fortress. Another, more prosaic version, says that he wormed his way into the confidence of the commandant, became his right-hand man, and succeeded him on his death. A little later the Ismailis gained a second castle near Isfahan, called Khalinjan – whether by capture or cession is not clear. A tale of the kind that the chroniclers delight in telling about the Ismailis has it that a carpenter made friends with the commander and gave a banquet at which he got the whole garrison blind drunk.

Sultan Berkyaruq, who had succeeded Malikshah in 1092, was fully occupied with his struggle against his half-brother Muhammad Tapar, supported by the latter's full brother Sanjar. At best, the Sultan had little attention and few forces to spare for the Ismailis; at worst, he or some of his lieutenants were ready to tolerate Ismaili action against his enemies and even perhaps, on occasion, discreetly to seek their help. Thus, Berkyaruq's representatives in Khurasan enlisted the support of the Ismailis of Quhistan against the rival faction. In the assassins' roll of honour in the chronicles of Alamut, nearly fifty assassinations are recorded during the reign of Hasan-i Sabbah, beginning with Nizam al-Mulk. More than half of them belong to this period – and some of the victims, it was said, were supporters of Muhammad Tapar and opponents of Berkyaruq.

In the summer of 1100 Berkyaruq inflicted a defeat on Muhammad Tapar, who had to retreat to Khurasan. Following this victory, the Ismailis became bolder and more self-assertive, and even infiltrated Berkyaruq's court and army. They won over many of the troops, and threatened those who opposed them with assassination. 'No commander or officer,' says the Arabic chronicler, 'dared to leave his house unprotected; they wore armour under clothes, and even the vizier Abu'l-Hasan wore a mail shirt under his clothes. Sultan Berkyaruq's high officers asked him for permission to appear before him armed, for fear of attack, and he granted them permission.'[24]

The growing menace and insolence of the Ismailis, and the mounting anger of his own supporters at his complacency or worse, at last forced Berkyaruq to take action. In 1101 he seems to have reached an agreement with Sanjar, who was still ruling in Khurasan, for combined action against an enemy who threatened both of them. Sanjar sent a large and well-armed expedition, commanded by his senior emir, against the Ismaili areas in Quhistan, where they devastated the countryside and then laid siege to Tabas, the main Ismaili stronghold. Using mangonels, they destroyed most of the walls and were on the point of capturing it, when the Ismailis bribed the emir to raise the siege and go away. They were then able to repair, refortify and reinforce Tabas, to meet the next attack. This came three years later, when the emir led a new army to Quhistan, including, in addition to his own regulars, a number of volunteers. This time their campaign was successful, but curiously inconclusive. The Seljuq troops conquered and destroyed Tabas and other Ismaili castles, pillaged the Ismaili settlements and enslaved some of their inhabitants – and then withdrew, after exacting a pledge from the Ismailis that 'they would not build a castle, nor buy arms, nor summon any to their faith'.[25] There were many who thought these terms far too lenient, and censured Sanjar for accepting them. Sure enough, it was not very long before the Ismailis were once again solidly established in Quhistan.

In Western Persia and Iraq Berkyaruq made no real effort to attack the centres of Ismaili power. Instead, he tried to appease the anger of his officers and of the populace by permitting or encouraging a massacre of Ismaili sympathizers in Isfahan. Soldiers and citizens joined in the hunt for suspects, who were rounded up, taken to the great square, and killed. A simple accusation was enough, and many innocents, says Ibn al-Athir, died by private vengeance on that day. From Isfahan, the anti-Ismaili action was extended to Iraq, where Ismailis were killed in the camp at Baghdad, and Ismaili books were burnt. One prominent Ismaili, Abu Ibrahim Asadabadi, had been sent to Baghdad by the Sultan

himself on an official mission. The Sultan now sent orders for
his arrest. When his jailers came to kill him, Asadabadi said:
'Very well, you have killed me – but can you kill those who are
in the castles?'[26]

Asadabadi's taunt was to the point. The Ismailis had suffered
a setback; they could no longer count on the acquiescence of
Berkyaruq and for a while the fida'is were comparatively inactive – but their castles remained inviolate, and their reign of
terror, though curbed, was by no means at an end. Between 1101
and 1103, the roll of honour records the murder of the Mufti
of Isfahan in the old mosque of that city, the prefect of Bayhaq,
and the chief of the Karramiyya, a militant anti-Ismaili religious
order, in the mosque of Nishapur. The murder of Seljuq officers
and officials had, it would seem, for the moment become too
difficult – but there was still the task of punishing those civil and
religious dignitaries who had dared to oppose the Ismailis. It was
during these years that the ruler of Alamut took another important
step – the despatch of missionaries to Syria.

The Ismaili menace to the Seljuq Empire had been contained
but not destroyed. After the death of Berkyaruq in 1105 his successor Muhammad Tapar made a new and determined effort to
overcome them. 'When the Sultanate was firmly in the hands of
Muhammad and no rival remained to dispute it with him, he
had no more urgent task than to seek out and fight the Ismailis
and to avenge the Muslims for their oppression and misdeeds.
He decided to begin with the castle of Isfahan which was in their
hands, for this was the most troublesome and dominated his
capital city. So he led his army against them in person, and laid
siege to them on the 6th Sha'ban 500 [2 April 1107].'[27]

The siege and conquest of the castle were delayed by a series
of tricks and manoeuvres, arranged by the Ismailis and their
friends. At the very beginning, the departure of the expedition
had been postponed for five weeks, as a result of false reports
of dangers elsewhere, put about by Ismaili sympathizers in the
Sultan's camp. When the local Ismaili leader Ahmad ibn Attāsh
found himself hard pressed, he gained a breathing spell by starting a religious controversy. In a message to the Sultan, the

Ismailis claimed that they were good Muslims, believers in God and the Prophet, observers of the Holy Law. They differed from the Sunnis only concerning the Imamate, and it would therefore be proper for the Sultan to grant them a truce and terms, and accept their allegiance. This initiated a religious debate – between the attackers and the defenders, and between different schools of thought in the attacking camp. Many of the Sultan's theological advisers were willing to accept the Ismaili argument, but a few stood firm for a more rigorous attitude. 'Let them answer this question,' said one of them. ' "If your Imam were to permit you what the Holy Law forbids, and forbid you what the Holy Law permits, would you obey him?" If they answer yes, their blood is lawful.' Thanks to the insistence of the rigorists, the debate came to nothing, and the siege continued.

The Ismailis now tried a different tack, proposing a compromise whereby they would be given another fortress in the vicinity, 'for the protection of their lives and property from the mob'. Negotiations dragged on, while the Sultan's vizier himself arranged for supplies of food to be sent into the fortress. This phase ended when an Ismaili assassin wounded but failed to kill one of the Sultan's emirs who had been particularly outspoken against them. The Sultan now pressed the siege again, and the only hope that remained to the defenders was a negotiated surrender.

Before long, terms were agreed. Part of the garrison was to be allowed to leave and go, under the Sultan's protection, to the Ismaili centres at Tabas and near Arrajan. The remainder were to move into one wing of the fortress and abandon the rest to the Sultan. When news was received of the safe arrival of their comrades, they too would come down, and would be permitted to go to Alamut. In due course news was received of the arrival of those who had left, but Ibn Attāsh declined to fulfil his part of the bargain. Taking advantage of the respite, he had concentrated his arms and men – some eighty of them – in the remaining wing of the fortress, and prepared for a fight to the death. They were overcome only when a traitor pointed out that on one wall there was only a row of weapons and armour, arranged to look like men – but no men. In the final assault most of the defenders perished. Ibn Attāsh's wife threw herself down from the ramparts, decked in her jewels, and was killed; Ibn Attāsh was captured and paraded through the streets of Isfahan. He was then flayed alive – his skin stuffed with straw, his head sent to Baghdad.

In a victory-letter, published to celebrate this triumph, the Sultan's secretary gives, in the somewhat pompous style usual in these documents, a Seljuq view of the enemy that they had overcome: 'In this castle of Shahdiz . . . falsehood was laid and hatched . . . there was Ibn Attāsh, whose reason flew away on the path of error and went astray, who told men that the Way of Right Guidance was a false track, and took as his guide a book loaded with lies, and gave licence to shed the blood and leave to take the property of the Muslims. . . . Even had they done no more than what they did when first they came to Isfahan – in treacherously tracking and cunningly catching their quarry, and killing them with terrible tortures and a dreadful death, in multiple murder beginning with the notables of the court and the elite of the Ulema, in shedding more than can be counted or measured of inviolable blood, and other offences vexatious to Islam . . . it would have been our duty to fight in defence of religion, and ride both the docile and the headstrong steed in holy warfare against them, even as far as China . . .'[28]

China was of course no more than a stylistic flourish – an allusion to a well-known saying of the Prophet. But the Sultan's attack on the Ismailis extended to both the eastern and western extremities of the Seljuq Empire. In Iraq, an expedition against Takrit, which the Ismailis had held for twelve years, failed to capture the place, but forced the Ismaili commandant to hand it over to local Arab Shi'ites. In the East, Sanjar was urged to take action against the Ismaili bases in Quhistan, though with what effect is not clear. At about this time, or shortly after, the Ismaili strongholds near Arrajan were overcome, and little more is heard of them in the region of Khuzistan and Fars.

But the main centre of Ismaili power was in none of these places. It was in the north – in the castles of Rudbar and Girdkuh, and above all in the great fortress of Alamut, the residence of Hasan-i Sabbah. In 1107–8 the Sultan sent a military expedition to Rudbar, under the direction of his vizier Ahmad ibn Nizam al-Mulk. The vizier had his own good reasons for hating the Ismailis. His father, the famous Nizam al-Mulk, had been the first of their great victims; his brother, Fakhr al-Mulk, had fallen to the dagger of an assassin in Nishapur in the previous year.

The expedition gained some successes and inflicted great hardship on the Ismailis, but failed to achieve its purpose – the capture or destruction of Alamut. 'He [Ahmad b. Nizam al-Mulk] encompassed Alamut and Ustavand, which is near to it on the banks of the Andij, and they waged war for some time and destroyed the crops. Then, being unable to accomplish more, the army departed from Rudbar. In their castles there was a great famine and the people lived on grass; and it was for this reason that they sent their wives and children elsewhere and he [Hasan-i Sabbah] too sent his wife and daughters to Girdkuh.'[29]

Besides sending his own regular troops, the Sultan also tried to raise the immediate neighbours of the Ismailis against them, and prevailed on a local ruler in Gilan to join in the attack – but to no purpose. Later the local ruler, allegedly antagonized by the Sultan's arrogance, withheld his support. He may have had other reasons. The predicament of the local rulers of Daylam, between their terrible and near neighbours and their powerful but remote overlords, is vividly described by Juvayni: 'On this account the local rulers, near and far, were exposed to danger, whether their friends or their foes, and would fall into the whirlpool of destruction – their friends, because the kings of Islam would subdue and destroy them and they would suffer "the loss of this world and the next" [Qur'an, xxii, 11]; while their foes for fear of his guile and treachery would flee into the cage of defence and precaution and [even so] were mostly killed.'[30]

The capture of Alamut by direct assault was clearly impossible. The Sultan therefore tried another method – a war of attrition which, it was hoped, would weaken the Ismailis to the point where they could no longer resist attack. 'For eight consecutive years', says Juvayni, 'the troops came to Rudbar and destroyed the crops, and the two sides were engaged in battle. When it was known that Hasan and his men were left without strength or food, [Sultan Muhammad] at the beginning of the year 511/1117–18, appointed the *atabeg* Nushtegin Shirgir as commander of the troops and ordered him to lay siege to the castles from then onwards. On the 1st of Safar [4 June 1117] they invested Lamasar and on the 11th of Rabi' 1 [13 July] Alamut. Setting up their mangonels they fought strenuously and by Dhu'l–Hijja of that year [March–April 1118] were on the point of taking the castles and freeing mankind from their machinations, when they received news that Sultan Muhammad had died in Isfahan. The troops then dispersed, and the Heretics were left alive and dragged up into their castles all the stores, arms and implements of war assembled by the Sultan's army.'[31]

The withdrawal of Shirgir's army, when on the point of victory, was a profound disappointment. There are some indications that it was not only the news of the Sultan's death that caused their hurried departure. A sinister role is attributed to one Qiwam al-Din Nasir b. 'Ali al-Dargazini, a vizier in the Seljuq service, and, it was alleged, a secret Ismaili. He had great influence over Sultan Muhammad's son Mahmud who succeeded him as Sultan in Isfahan, and played a role of some importance at his court. He is said to have procured the withdrawal of Shirgir's army from Alamut, thus rescuing the Ismailis, and to have poisoned the new Sultan's mind against Shirgir, who was imprisoned and put to death. Later, al-Dargazini was accused of complicity in several other murders.[32]

Even while under attack, the assassins were not idle. In 1108–9 they killed Ubayd Allah al-Khatib, a Qadi of Isfahan, and a whole-hearted opponent of the Ismailis. The Qadi knew the risks. He wore armour, had a bodyguard, and took precautions – but to no avail. During the Friday prayers in the mosque of Hamadan an assassin got between him and his bodyguard and struck him down. In the same year the Qadi of Nishapur was murdered during the celebrations at the end of Ramadan. In Baghdad, an assassin fell upon Ahmad b. Nizam al-Mulk, no doubt to punish him for leading an expedition to Alamut; the vizier was wounded, but survived. There were other victims too – Sunni divines and jurists, and great dignitaries such as the Kurdish emir Ahmadil, the foster-brother of the Sultan.

The death of Sultan Muhammad in 1118 was followed by another interval of internecine conflict among the Seljuqs, during which the Assassins were able to recover from the blows which they had suffered and to restore their position in both Quhistan and the North. In time Sanjar, who had controlled the eastern provinces under his brothers Berkyaruq and Mohammad Tapar, managed to establish a precarious primacy among Seljuq rulers. In this period the nature of relations between the Ismailis and the Sunni states begins to change. The ultimate aims of the Ismaili movement are not renounced, but the Ismaili campaign of subversion and terror in the central lands is muted; instead, they concentrate on defending and consolidating the territories which they control, and even acquire some measure of political recognition. At a time when the fragmentation of the Middle East, interrupted by the great Seljuq conquests, was being resumed, the Ismaili principalities and seignories take their place in the pattern of small independent states, and even participate in local alliances and rivalries.

A story told by Juvayni explains the tolerance of Sanjar towards Ismaili independence: 'Hasan-i Sabbah would send ambassadors to seek peace but his offers were not accepted. He then by all manner of wiles bribed certain of the Sultan's courtiers to defend him before the Sultan; and he suborned one of his eunuchs with a large sum of money and sent him a dagger, which was stuck in the ground beside the Sultan's bed one night when he lay in drunken sleep. When the Sultan awoke and saw the dagger he was filled with alarm but not knowing whom to suspect he ordered the matter to be kept secret. Hasan-i Sabbah then sent a messenger with the following message: "Did I not wish the Sultan well that dagger which was struck into the hard ground would have been planted in his soft breast." The Sultan took fright and from then on inclined towards peace with them. In short, because of this imposture the Sultan refrained from attacking them and during his reign their cause prospered. He allowed them a pension of 3,000 dinars from the taxes on the lands belonging to them in the region of Qumish and also permitted them to levy a small toll on travellers passing beneath Girdkuh, a custom which has survived to this day. I saw several of Sanjar's firmans which had been preserved in their library and in which he conciliated and flattered them; and from these I was able to deduce the extent to which the Sultan connived at their actions and sought to be on peaceful terms with them. In short, during his reign they enjoyed ease and tranquillity.'[33]

The Nizaris of Alamut had another enemy, besides the Abbasid Caliphs and the Seljuq Sultans. In Cairo there was still a Fatimid Caliph, and between his followers and the Nizaris of Persia there was that special, intimate hatred that exists between rival branches of the same religion. In 1121 the redoubtable al-Afdal, the vizier and Commander of the Armies, was murdered in Cairo. Rumour inevitably blamed the Assassins – but a contemporary Damascene chronicler describes this as 'empty pretence and insubstantial calumny'.[34] The real reason for the murder, he says, was an estrangement between al-Afdal and the Fatimid Caliph al-Amir, who had succeeded al-Musta'li in 1101. Al-Amir had resented the tutelage of his powerful vizier, and openly rejoiced at his death. This might well be, but rumour, this time, was right. The Ismaili narrative cited by Rashid al-Din and Kashani credits the murder to 'three comrades from Aleppo'. When news came of Afdal's death, 'Our Master ordered them to celebrate for seven days and nights, and they entertained and feted the comrades.'[35]

The removal of al-Afdal, which caused such joy both in the castle of Alamut and the palace of Cairo, seemed a good moment to attempt a rapprochement between the two branches. In 1122 a public assembly was held in Cairo, at which the case for Musta'li and against Nizar was recited and demonstrated; at about the same time, the Caliph defended his legitimacy in a pastoral letter, addressed primarily to the separated brethren, and the new vizier in Cairo, al-Ma'mun, instructed the secretary of chancery to write a long letter to Hasan-i Sabbah, urging him to return to the truth and to renounce his belief in the Imamate of Nizar.

Thus far al-Ma'mun – himself a Twelver and not an Ismaili
Shi'ite – complied with the wishes of the Caliph and the da'is.
But the vizier clearly had no intention of allowing these dealings
with Hasan-i Sabbah to go too far. The alleged discovery of
a plot, directed and financed from Alamut, to assassinate both
al-Amir and al-Ma'mun, was followed by the most elaborate
security precautions, at the frontiers and in Cairo, to prevent
the infiltration of assassin agents. 'When al-Ma'mun came to
power, it was reported to him that Ibn al-Sabbah [i.e. Hasan-i
Sabbah] and the Batinis rejoiced at the death of al-Afdal, and
that their hopes extended to the murder of both al-Amir and
al-Ma'mun himself, and that they had sent messengers to their
comrades living in Egypt, with money to distribute among
them.

'Al-Ma'mun came to the governor of Asqalan, and dismissed
him, and appointed another in his place. He ordered the new
governor to parade and inspect all holders of offices in Asqalan,
and to remove all but those who were known to the local population. He instructed him to make a thorough examination of all
merchants and other persons who arrived there, and not to take
on trust what they themselves said as to their names, by-names
and countries . . . but to question them about one another and to
deal with them separately and to devote the greatest care to all
this. If anyone came who was not in the habit of coming, he was
to stop him at the border, and investigate his circumstances and
the goods he was carrying. He was to deal in the same way with
the camel-drivers, and to deny entry to the country to all save
those who were known and regular visitors. He was not to
allow any caravan to proceed until after he had sent a report in
writing to the *diwan*, stating the number of merchants, their
names, the names of their servants, the names of the camel-
drivers, and a list of their merchandise, to be checked at the
city of Bilbays and on their arrival at the gate. At the same time
he was to show honour to the merchants and refrain from vexing
them.

'Then orders came from al-Ma'mun to the governors of
old and new Cairo to register the names of all the inhabitants,

street by street and quarter by quarter, and not to permit any-one to move from one house to another without his express authorization.

'When he had taken note of the registers, and the names of the people of old and new Cairo, and their by-names and circum-stances and livelihoods, and of whatever strangers came to each inhabitant of the quarters, then he sent out women to enter these houses and to pursue enquiries about the affairs of the Ismailis, so that there was nothing concerning the affairs of anyone in old or new Cairo that was hidden from him ... then one day he sent out a number of soldiers and scattered them, and ordered them to arrest those whom he indicated ...'[36] Many such agents were arrested, including the tutor of the Caliph's children; some of them had money in their possession, which Hasan-i Sabbah had given them for use in Egypt. So successful were the vizier's policemen and spies, says the Egyptian chronicler, that from the very moment when an assassin left Alamut his movements were known and reported. A letter of pardon, inviting the Nizari leaders by name to return to the fold without fear of punishment, was apparently never sent, and relations between Cairo and Alamut deteriorated rapidly.

In May 1124 Hasan-i Sabbah fell ill. Feeling that his end was near, he made arrangements for his succession. His chosen heir was Buzurgumid, for 20 years commandant of Lammasar. 'He sent someone to Lamasar to fetch Buzurgumid, and appointed him his successor. And he made Dihdar Abu-Ali of Ardistan [sit] on his right and entrusted him in particular with the propa-ganda chancery; Hasan son of Adam of Qasran he made [sit] on his left and Kya Ba-Ja'far, who was the commander of his forces, in front of him. And he charged them, until such time as the Imam came to take possession of his kingdom, to act all four in concert and agreement. And in the night of Wednesday the 6th of Rabi' II, 518 [Friday, 23 May 1124], he hastened off to the fire of God and His hell.'[37]

It was the end of a remarkable career. An Arabic biographer, by no means friendly, describes him as 'perspicacious, capable, learned in geometry, arithmetic, astronomy, magic, and other things'.[38] The Ismaili biography cited by the Persian chroniclers stresses his asceticism and abstinence – 'during the 35 years that he dwelt in Alamut nobody drank wine openly or put it in jars.'[39] His severity was not confined to his opponents. One of his sons was executed for drinking wine; another was put to death on a charge, subsequently proved false, of having procured the murder of the da'i Husayn Qa'ini. 'And he used to point to the execution of both his sons as a reason against any one's imagining that he had conducted propaganda on their behalf and had had that object in mind.'[40]

Hasan-i Sabbah was a thinker and writer as well as a man of action. Sunni authors have preserved two citations from his works – a fragment of an autobiography, and an abridgement of a theological treatise.[41] Among later Ismailis, he was revered as the prime mover in the *da'wa jadida* – new preaching – the reformed Ismaili doctrine which was promulgated after the break with Cairo, and which was preserved and elaborated among the Nizari Ismailis. Later Nizari works contain a number of passages which may be quotations or summaries of his own teachings. Hasan never claimed to be an Imam – only a representative of the Imam. After the disappearance of the Imam he was the *Hujja*, the proof – the source of knowledge of the hidden Imam of his time, the living link between the lines of manifest Imams of the past and the future, and the leader of the *da'wa*. Ismaili doctrine is basically authoritarian. The believer has no right of choice, but must follow the *ta'lim*, the authorized teaching. The ultimate source of guidance was the Imam; the immediate source was his accredited representative. Men could not choose their Imam, as the Sunnis said, nor exercise judgement in determining the truth in matters of theology and law. God appointed the Imam, and the Imam was the repository of the truth. Only the Imam could validate both revelation and reason; only the Ismaili Imam, by the nature of his office and teaching, could in fact do this, and he alone therefore was the true Imam. His rivals were usurpers, their followers sinners, their teachings falsehood.

This doctrine, with its stress on loyalty and obedience, and its rejection of the world as it was, became a powerful weapon in the hands of a secret, revolutionary opposition. The painful realities of the Fatimid Caliphate in Egypt had become an embarrassment to Ismaili claims. The break with Cairo, and the transfer of allegiance to a mysterious hidden Imam, released the pent-up forces of Ismaili passion and devotion; it was the achievement of Hasan-i Sabbah to arouse and direct them.

4

The Mission in Persia

The death of a Seljuq Sultan meant an immediate halt to all positive action, and an interval of conflict and uncertainty, during which the internal and external enemies of the state could find and seize their opportunities. There must have been many who expected that the Ismaili principality founded by Hasan-i Sabbah would, on his death, conform to this lamentably normal pattern of Muslim government in this period.

In 1126, two years after the succession of Buzurgumid, Sultan Sanjar launched an attack which put the question to the test. Since his expedition against Tabas in 1103, Sanjar had taken no action against the Ismailis, and may even have entered into some sort of agreement with them. No immediate *casus belli* for the anti-Ismaili offensive of 1126 is known. The growing confidence of the Sultan, and the presumed weakness of the Ismailis under their new ruler, may be a sufficient explanation of his decision no longer to tolerate this dangerous and independent power on the borders and even within the borders of his Empire. An important role was played by the Sultan's vizier Mu'in al-Din Kashi, an advocate of strong action.

The first attack seems to have come in the East. 'In this year the vizier ... gave orders to make war against the Ismailis, to kill them wherever they were and wherever they were conquered, to pillage their property and enslave their women. He sent an army against Turaythith [in Quhistan] which was in their hands, and against Bayhaq, in the province of Nishapur ... he despatched troops against every part of their possessions, with orders to kill whatever Ismailis they encountered.'[1] The implication would seem to be that the Ismailis were to be denied the rights allowed to prisoners and civilians by Muslim law in inter-Muslim warfare, and to be treated as infidels, subject to death or enslavement. The Arabic chronicler reports two successes – the conquest of the Ismaili village of Tarz, near Bayhaq, where the population was put to the sword and their leader killed himself by leaping from the minaret of the mosque, and a raid on Turaythith, where the troops 'killed many, took much booty, and then returned'. It is clear that the results of the campaign were limited and inconclusive. In the north the offensive fared even worse. An expedition against Rudbar, led by the nephew of Shirgir, was driven back, and much booty taken from them. Another, launched with local help, was also defeated, and one of its commanders captured.

The vengeance of the Ismailis was not long delayed. Two fida'is wormed their way into the vizier's household in the guise of grooms, and by their skill and their display of piety gained his confidence. They found their opportunity when the vizier summoned them to his presence, to choose two Arab horses as a gift for the Sultan on the Persian New Year. The murder took place on 16 March 1127. 'He did good deeds and showed worthy intentions in fighting against them,' said Ibn al-Athir, 'and God granted him martyrdom.'[2] The same historian records a punitive expedition by Sanjar against Alamut, in which more than 10,000 Ismailis perished. This is not mentioned by Ismaili or other sources, and is probably an invention.

The end of hostilities found the Ismailis rather stronger than before. In Rudbar, they had reinforced their position by building a new and powerful fortress, called Maymundiz,[3] and had extended their territory, notably by acquiring Talaqan. In the East, Ismaili forces, presumably from Quhistan, raided Sistan in 1129.[4] In the same year Mahmud, the Seljuq Sultan of Isfahan, found it prudent to discuss peace, and invited an envoy from Alamut. Unfortunately the envoy, with a colleague, was lynched by the Isfahan mob when he left the Sultan's presence. The Sultan apologized and disclaimed responsibility but, understandably, refused Buzurgumid's request to punish the murderers. The Ismailis responded by attacking Qazvin, where, according to their own chronicle, they killed four hundred people and took enormous booty. The Qazvinis tried to fight back, but, says the Ismaili chronicler, when the comrades killed one Turkish emir, the rest of them fled.[5] An attack on Alamut by Mahmud himself at this time failed to achieve any result.

In 1131 Sultan Mahmud died, and the usual wrangle followed between his brothers and his son. Some of the emirs managed to involve the Caliph of Baghdad, al-Mustarshid, in an alliance against Sultan Mas'ud, and in 1139 the Caliph, with his vizier and a number of his dignitaries, was captured by Mas'ud near Hamadan. The Sultan took his distinguished captive to Maragha, where he is said to have treated him with respect – but did not prevent a large group of Ismailis from entering the camp and murdering him. An Abbasid Caliph – the titular head of Sunni Islam – was an obvious objective for the daggers of the assassins if opportunity arose, but rumour accused Mas'ud of complicity or deliberate negligence, and even charged Sanjar, still the nominal overlord of the Seljuq rulers, as an instigator of the crime. Juvayni tries hard to exonerate both of them from these charges: 'Some of the more short-sighted and ill-wishers to the House of Sanjar accused them of responsibility for this act. But "the astrologers lied, by the Lord of the Ka'ba!" The goodness of Sultan Sanjar's character and the purity of his nature as instanced in his following and strengthening the Hanafite faith and the Shari'a [holy law], his respect for all that related to the Caliphate as also his mercy and compassion are too plain and evident for the like false and slanderous charges to be laid against his person, which was the source of clemency and the fountain-head of pity.'[6]

In Alamut, the news of the Caliph's death was received with exultation. They celebrated for seven days and nights, made much of the comrades, and reviled the name and emblems of the Abbasids.

The list of assassinations in Persia during the reign of Buzurgumid is comparatively short, though not undistinguished. Besides the Caliph, the victims include a prefect of Isfahan, a governor of Maragha, murdered not long before the arrival of the Caliph in that city, a prefect of Tabriz, and a mufti of Qazvin.

The slackening in the pace of assassination is not the only change in the character of the Ismaili principality. Unlike Hasan-i Sabbah, Buzurgumid was a local man in Rudbar, not a stranger; he had not shared Hasan's experience as a secret agitator, but had spent most of his active life as a ruler and administrator. His adoption of the role of a territorial ruler, and his acceptance by others as such, are strikingly demonstrated by the flight to Alamut, with his followers, of the emir Yarankush, an old and redoubtable enemy of the Ismailis, when he was displaced by the rising power of the Khorazmshah (Shah of Khorazm). The Shah asked for their surrender, arguing that he had been a friend of the Ismailis, while Yarankush had been their enemy – but Buzurgumid refused to hand them over, saying: 'I cannot reckon as an enemy anyone who places himself under my protection.'[7] The Ismaili chronicler of the reign of Buzurgumid takes an obvious delight in recounting such stories of magnanimity – stories that reflect the role of a chivalrous lord rather than a revolutionary leader.

The Ismaili ruler fulfilled this role even to the point of suppressing heresy. In 1131, says the Ismaili chronicler, a Shiʻite called Abu Hashim appeared in Daylam and sent letters as far away as Khurasan. 'Buzurgumid sent him a letter of advice, drawing his attention to the proofs of God.' Abu Hashim replied: 'What you say is unbelief and heresy. If you come here and we discuss it, the falsity of your beliefs will become apparent.' The Ismailis sent an army against him, and defeated him. 'They caught Abu Hashim, supplied him with ample proof, and burned him.'[8]

The long reign of Buzurgumid ended with his death on 9 February 1138. As Juvayni elegantly puts it: 'Buzurgumid remained seated on the throne of Ignorance ruling over Error until the 26th of Jumada I, 532 [9 February 1138], when he was crushed under the heel of Perdition and Hell was heated with the fuel of his carcase.'[9] It is significant of the changing nature of Ismaili leadership that he was succeeded without incident by his son Muhammad, whom he had nominated as heir only three days before his death. When Buzurgumid died, says the Ismaili chronicler, 'their enemies became joyful and insolent',[10] but they were soon made to realize that their hopes were vain.

The first victim of the new reign was another Abbasid – the ex-Caliph al-Rashid, the son and successor of the murdered al-Mustarshid. Like his father, he had become involved in Seljuq disputes, and had been solemnly deposed by an assembly of judges and jurists convened by the Sultan. Al-Rashid had then left Iraq for Persia, to join his allies, and was in Isfahan, recuperating from an illness, when his assassins found him on 5 or 6 June 1138. The murderers were Khurasanis in his own service. The death of a caliph was again celebrated with a week of rejoicing at Alamut, in honour of the first 'victory' of the new reign.[11]

The role of honour for the reign of Muhammad lists in all fourteen assassinations. Besides the Caliph, the most notable victim was the Seljuq Sultan Da'ud, murdered by four Syrian assassins in Tabriz in 1143. It was alleged that the murderers had been sent by Zangi, the ruler of Mosul, who was expanding his realm into Syria and feared that Da'ud might be sent to replace him. It is certainly curious that a murder in North Western Persia should have been arranged from Syria and not from near-by Alamut. Other victims include an emir at Sanjar's court and one of his associates, a prince of the house of the Khorazmshahs, local rulers in Georgia (?) and Mazandaran, a vizier, and the Qadis of Quhistan, Tiflis and Hamadan, who had authorized or instigated the killing of Ismailis.

It was a meagre haul compared with the great days of Hasan-i Sabbah, and reflects the growing concern of the Ismailis with local and territorial problems. In the Ismaili chronicle these take pride of place. The great affairs of the Empire are hardly mentioned; instead, there are circumstantial accounts of local conflicts with neighbouring rulers, embellished with lists of the cows, sheep, asses and other booty taken. The Ismailis more than held their own in a series of raids and counter-raids between Rudbar and Qazvin, and in 1143 repelled an attack by Sultan Mahmud on

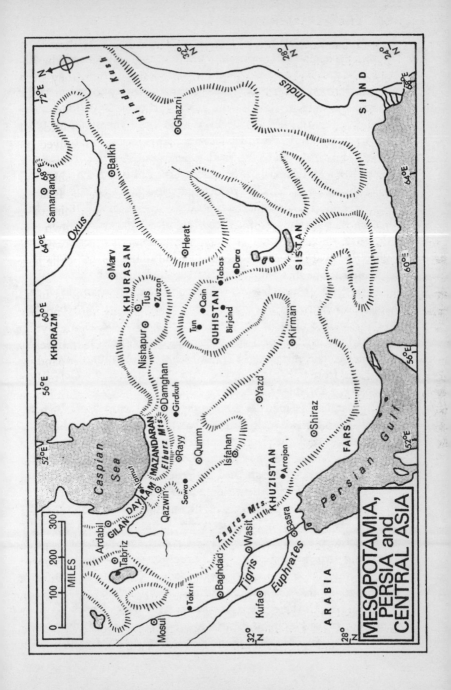

Alamut. They managed to gain or build some new fortresses in the Caspian districts, and are even reported to have extended their activities to two new areas – in Georgia, where they raided and carried on propaganda, and in present-day Afghanistan, where they were invited by the ruler, for reasons of his own, to send a mission. On his death in 1161 both missionaries and converts were put to death by his successor.

Two enemies were specially persistent – the ruler of Mazandaran, and Abbas, the Seljuq governor of Rayy, who organized a massacre of Ismailis in that city and attacked the Ismaili territories. Both are said to have built towers of Ismaili skulls. In 1146 or 1147 Abbas was murdered by Sultan Mas'ud while on a visit to Baghdad, 'on a sign', says the Ismaili chronicler, 'from Sultan Sanjar'.[12] His head was sent to Khurasan. There are several such indications that Sanjar and the Ismailis are on the same side, though at other times they came into conflict, as for example when Sanjar supported an attempt to restore the Sunni faith in one of the Ismaili centres in Quhistan. There as elsewhere, the issues involved are usually local and territorial. It is noteworthy that in the other Ismaili castles and seignories, besides Alamut, leadership descended from father to son, and often the conflicts in which they are engaged are purely dynastic.

The passion seemed to have gone out of Ismailism. In the virtual stalemate and tacit mutual acceptance between the Ismaili principalities and the Sunni monarchies, the great struggle to overthrow the old order and establish a new millennium, in the name of the hidden Imam, had dwindled into border-squabbles and cattle-raids. The castle strongholds, originally intended to be the spearheads of a great onslaught on the Sunni Empire, had become the centres of local sectarian dynasties, of a type not uncommon in Islamic history. The Ismailis even had their own mint, and struck their own coins. True, the fida'is still practised murder, but this was not peculiar to them, and in any case hardly sufficed to fire the hopes of the faithful.

Among them there were still some who harked back to the glorious days of Hasan-i Sabbah – to the dedication and adventure of his early struggles, and the religious faith that inspired them.

They found a leader in Hasan, the son and heir apparent of the lord of Alamut, Muhammad. His interest began early. 'When he had nearly approached the age of discretion he conceived the desire to study and examine the teachings of Hasan-i Sabbah and his own forefathers; and ... he came to excel in the exposition of their creed ... With ... the eloquence of his words he won over the greater part of that people. Now his father being altogether lacking in that art, his son ... appeared a great scholar beside him, and therefore ... the vulgar sought to follow his lead. And not having heard the like discourses from his father they began to think that here was the Imam that had been promised by Hasan-i Sabbah. The people's attachment to him increased and they made haste to follow him as their leader.'

Muhammad did not like this at all. A conservative in his Ismailism, 'he was rigid in his observance of the principles laid down by his father and Hasan[-i Sabbah] with regard to the conduct of propaganda on behalf of the Imam and the outward observance of Muslim practices; and he considered his son's behaviour to be inconsistent with those principles. He therefore denounced him roundly and having assembled the people spoke as follows: "This Hasan is my son, and I am not the Imam but one of his da'is. Whoever listens to these words and believes them is an infidel and atheist." And on these grounds he punished some who had believed in his son's Imamate with all manner of tortures and torments, and on one occasion put 250 persons to death on Alamut and then binding their corpses on the backs of 250 others condemned on the same charge he expelled these latter from the castle. And in this way they were discouraged and suppressed.'[13] Hasan bided his time, and managed to dispel his father's suspicions. On Muhammad's death in 1162 he succeeded him without opposition. He was then about 35 years old.

Hasan's rule was at first uneventful, marked only by a certain relaxation in the rigorous enforcement of the Holy Law that had previously been maintained at Alamut. Then, two and a half years after his accession, in the middle of the fasting month of Ramadan, he proclaimed the millennium.

Ismaili accounts of what happened are preserved in the later literature of the sect and also, in a somewhat modified form, in the Persian chronicles written after the fall of Alamut. They tell a curious tale. On the 17th day of the month of Ramadan, of the year 559 [8 August 1164], under the ascendancy of Virgo and when the sun was in Cancer, Hasan ordered the erection of a pulpit in the courtyard of Alamut, facing towards the west, with four great banners of four colours, white, red, yellow, and green, at the four corners. The people from the different regions, whom he had previously summoned to Alamut, were assembled in the courtyard – those from the East on the right side, those from the West on the left side, and those from the North, from Rudbar and Daylam, in front, facing the pulpit. As the pulpit faced west the congregants had their backs towards Mecca. 'Then,' says an Ismaili tract, 'towards noon, the Lord [Hasan], on his mention be peace, wearing a white garment and a white turban, came down from the castle, approached the pulpit from the right side, and in the most perfect manner ascended it. Three times he uttered greetings, first to the Daylamis, then to those on the right, then to those on the left. In a moment he sat down, and then rose up again and, holding his sword, spoke in a loud voice.' Addressing himself to 'the inhabitants of the worlds, *jinn*, men, and angels', he announced that a message had come to him from the hidden Imam, with new guidance. 'The Imam of our time has sent you his blessing and his compassion, and has called you his special chosen servants. He has freed you from the burden of the rules of Holy Law, and has brought you to the Resurrection.' In addition, the Imam named Hasan, the son of Muhammad, the son of Buzurgumid, as 'our vicar, da'i and proof. Our party must obey and follow him both in religious and worldly matters, recognize his commands as binding, and know that his word is our word.'[14] When he had completed his address, Hasan stepped down from the pulpit, and performed two prostrations of the festival prayer. Then, a table having been laid, he invited them to break their fast, join in a banquet, and make merry. Messengers were sent to carry the glad tidings to east and west. In Quhistan, the chief of the fortress of Mu'minabad repeated the ceremony of

Alamut, and proclaimed himself as the vicar of Hasan, from a pulpit facing the wrong way; 'And that day on which these ignominies were divulged and these evils proclaimed in that nest of heretics, Mu'minabad, that assembly played harp and rebeck and openly drank wine upon the very steps of that pulpit and within its precincts.'[15] In Syria too the word was received, and the faithful celebrated the end of the law.

The solemn and ritual violation of the law – the congregants with their backs towards Mecca, the afternoon banquet in the midst of the fast – mark the culmination of a millenarian and antinomian tendency which is recurrent in Islam, and has obvious parallels in Christendom. The law has served its purpose, and its reign is ended; the secrets are revealed, the grace of the Imam prevails. By making the faithful his chosen personal servants, he has preserved them from sin; by proclaiming the Resurrection, he has saved them from death, and brought them, living, to that spiritual Paradise which is the knowledge of the Truth, and the contemplation of the Divine Essence. 'Now the essence of this futile creed ... was that following the Philosophers they spoke of the world as being uncreated and Time as unlimited and the Resurrection as spiritual. And they explained paradise and hell ... in such a way as to give a spiritual meaning to these concepts. And then on the basis of this they said that the Resurrection is when men shall come to God and the mysteries and truths of all Creation be revealed, and acts of obedience abolished, for in this world all is action and there is no reckoning, but in the world to come all is reckoning and there is no action. And this is the spiritual [Resurrection] and the Resurrection promised and awaited in all religions and creeds is this, which was revealed by Hasan. And as a consequence hereof men have been relieved of the duties imposed by the Shari'a because in this period of the Resurrection they must turn in every sense towards God and abandon the rites of religious law and established habits of worship. It was laid down in the Shari'a that men must worship God five times a day and be with Him. That charge was only formal, but now in [the days of] the Resurrection they must always be with God in their hearts and keep the faces of their souls constantly turned in the direction of the Divine Presence for such is true prayer.'[16]

The new dispensation brought an important change in the status of the Lord of Alamut. In the sermon in the castle court-yard, he is declared to be the vicar of the Imam and the Living Proof; as the bringer of the Resurrection (*qiyāma*), he is the *Qā'im*, a dominating figure in Ismaili eschatology. According to Rashid al-Din, after his public manifestation Hasan circulated writings in which he said that, while outwardly he was known as the grandson of Buzurgumid, in the esoteric reality he was the Imam of the time, and the son of the previous Imam, of the line of Nizar. It is possible that, as some have argued, Hasan was not claiming physical descent from Nizar, which in the age of the Resurrection had ceased to signify, but a kind of spiritual filiation. There are indeed precedents in early Islamic messianic movements for such claims to spiritual or adoptive descent from the house of the Prophet. The later Ismaili tradition is, however, unanimous in asserting that Hasan and his descendants were of the true line of Nizar, though there are different versions as to how the substitution took place. Hasan himself is held in special vener-ation, and is always named as Hasan ala dhikrihi'l-salam – Hasan, 'on his mention be peace'.

Most of the Ismailis readily accepted the new dispensation. There were some, however, who refused to be delivered from the yoke of the law, and against them Hasan used the severest punishments to impose freedom. 'Hasan maintained both by implication and by clear declaration, that just as in the time of the Law if a man did not obey and worship but followed the rule of the Resurrection that obedience and worship are spiritual, he was punished and stoned and put to death, so now in the time of the Resurrection if a man complied with the letter of the Law and persisted in physical worship and rites, it was obligatory that he be chastised and stoned and put to death.'[17]

Among the recusants was Hasan's brother-in-law, the scion of a noble Daylami house. He, according to Juvayni, was one of 'those to the nostrils of whose hearts there still came some scent of piety and religion . . . This man was unable to endure the propagation of those shameful errors. God have mercy on him and reward him for the goodness of his intention! On Sunday the 6th Rabi‘ 1, 561 [9 January 1166] he stabbed the seducer Hasan in the castle of Lamasar and he departed from this world "unto God's burning fire".'¹⁸

Hasan was succeeded by his nineteen-year old son Muhammad, who proceeded to confirm that his father and therefore he himself were descendants of Nizar, and Imams. He is said to have been a prolific writer, and during his long reign the doctrine of the Resurrection was developed and elaborated – but it seems to have made remarkably little impact on the outside world. It is significant that the whole episode of the Resurrection at Alamut passed unmentioned in contemporary Sunni historiography, and only became known after the destruction of Alamut, when the writings of the Ismailis came into the hands of Sunni scholars.

Politically too, the reign of Muhammad II was uneventful. The men of Alamut continued to raid their neighbours, and the fida'is killed a vizier of the Caliph in Baghdad, but little else of significance happened. A story told by Rashid al-Din and other authors relates to the great Sunni theologian Fakhr al-Din Razi. In his lectures to theological students in Rayy, Fakhr al-Din made a special point of refuting and reviling the Ismailis. Hearing of this, the lord of Alamut decided to put a stop to it and sent a fida'i to Rayy. There he enrolled himself as a student, and attended Fakhr al-Din's lectures daily for seven months, until he found an opportunity of seeing his teacher alone in his room, on the pretext of discussing a knotty problem. The fida'i at once drew a knife, and menaced the theologian with it. 'Fakhr al-Din jumped aside, and said: "Man, what do you want?" The fida'i replied: "I want to slit your honour's belly from the breast to the navel, because you have cursed us from the pulpit."' After a tussle, the fida'i threw Fakhr al-Din to the ground, and sat on his chest. The terrified theologian promised to repent, and to refrain from such attacks in the future. The fida'i allowed himself to be persuaded, and, accepting a solemn undertaking from Fakhr al-Din to mend his ways, produced a bag containing 365 gold dinars. This, and a similar amount every year, would be paid to him in return for his compliance. Thenceforth, in his lectures on the sects of Islam, Fakhr al-Din took good care to avoid expressions offensive to the Ismailis. One of his students, noting this change, asked the reason for it. The professor replied: 'It is not advisable to curse the Ismailis, for they have both weighty and trenchant arguments.'[19] The story has the appearance of a fable – but it may be noted that in this writings Fakhr al-Din Razi, while not accepting the doctrines of the Ismailis, condemns one Sunni theologian for trying to refute them with fanatical and ill-informed abuse, and praises another for correctly citing an Ismaili text.[20] Razi's point, of course, is not that the Ismailis are right, but that theological controversy must be based on correct information and an intelligent understanding of an opponent's point of view.

In the meantime great political changes had been taking place in the eastern lands of Islam. The Seljuq Great Sultanate, which for a time had restored the unity and reaffirmed the purpose of Sunni Islam, was disintegrating; in its place a new pattern of principalities emerged, founded by Seljuqid princes or officers, and, to an increasing extent, by the chiefs of nomadic Turkoman tribes whom successive waves of Turkish migration had brought from Central Asia into the Middle East. The Turkish expansion had for the moment reached its territorial limits; the Turkish imperial structure of the Seljuqs had fallen in ruins – but Turkish penetration and colonization continued, deepening and strengthening the conquest that had already been achieved. Changes of régime brought no change of substance; the successor princes found it simpler to maintain the political, military and administrative practices of the Seljuqs, including their firm commitment to religious orthodoxy. Here and there, where Turks were few, local groups, of Persian, Kurdish or Arab origin, raised their heads and achieved some measure of independence – but in the main the Turkish chiefs, however divided by political allegiance, pursued their common aim of displacing and supplanting the old, native lords. In this they were largely successful.

Towards the end of the twelfth century a new power emerged in the East. South of the Aral Sea lay the land of Khorazm, seat of an old and prosperous civilization, protected by a cordon of deserts from the convulsions that were shaking the neighbouring countries. Like most of Central Asia, it had been conquered and colonized by Turks; its ruling dynasty was descended from a Turkish slave sent there as governor by the Seljuq Great Sultan Malikshah. These rulers had prospered, and had signalized their identification with the country which they ruled by adopting the old native title of Khorazmshah, Shah of Khorazm – at first as vassals of the great powers, then as independent rulers. Amid general chaos the prosperous and well-armed Khorazmian monarchy was a haven of security; it was not long before the monarch felt obliged to extend the benefits of his rule to other lands and peoples. In about 1190 the Khorazmshah Tekish occupied Khurasan, thus becoming master of eastern Iran, and a major power in Islam. The Caliph al-Nasir in Baghdad, hard-pressed by the last of the Seljuqs of Iran, Tughrul II, appealed to Tekish for help and thus provided the occasion for the Khorazmian armies to advance westwards, to the conquest of Rayy and Hamadan. It was at Rayy that, in 1194, the last of the Seljuqs was defeated and killed.

During the century and a half since the coming of the Seljuqs, the great Sultanate which they had established had become an accepted part of the Islamic pattern of authority. The death of the last Seljuq had thus created a vacancy – and the triumphant Khorazmshah was the obvious person to fill it. Tekish now sent a message to the Caliph al-Nasir, demanding that he accept and recognize him as Sultan in Baghdad. Al-Nasir, however, had other ideas – and Tekish, who had hoped to grow from the Caliph's ally to the Caliph's protector, found that instead he had become the Caliph's enemy.

Since the accession of al-Nasir in 1180, the Abbasid Caliphate had enjoyed a striking revival. For some three centuries the Caliphs had been little more than puppets – the nominal heads of Sunni Islam, but effectively under the domination of the military rulers, the emirs and later the sultans. The decay of Seljuq power in Iraq created an opportunity that al-Nasir was quick to seize. His aim was two-fold; to restore the religious unity of Islam and the moral authority of the Caliph as its head, and to establish a Caliphal principality in Iraq under the effective rule of the Caliph – a sort of state of the Church, free from any outside control or influence, to serve as the base for his religious policies. The second, and limited objective he pursued by political and military action, against Tughrul and later against Tekish; the first – and probably main – objective of an Islamic restoration was furthered by a series of religious, social and educational initiatives, including approaches to both the Twelver Shi'a and the Ismailis. With the second of these he achieved a surprising measure of success.

On 1 September 1210 the lord of Alamut, Muhammad 11, died, possibly of poison, and was succeeded by his son Jalal al-Din Hasan. Already during his father's lifetime, Hasan had shown signs of dissatisfaction with the doctrines and practices of the *qiyāma* and of a desire for acceptance in the larger brotherhood of Islam. 'During his childhood,' says Juvayni, 'his father had designated him as his successor. When he grew up and showed signs of intelligence, he rejected his father's creed and felt disgusted with the customs of heresy and libertinism. His father having guessed what his feelings were, a sort of hostility sprang up between them and they were apprehensive and mistrustful of one another ... Now Jalal al-Din Hasan, whether because of the orthodoxy of his beliefs or because of his hostility towards his father, conspired against Muhammad and sent secretly to the Caliph of Baghdad and the sultans and rulers of other lands to claim that, unlike his father, he was by faith a Muslim and that when his turn came to reign he would abolish the Heresy and reintroduce the observance of Islam ... From the very moment of his accession Jalal al-Din professed Islam, and severely rebuked his people and party for their adherence to the Heresy, and strictly forbade them continuing therein, urging them to adopt Islam and follow the rites of the Shari'a. He sent messengers to the Caliph of Baghdad, Muhammad Khorazmshah and the *maliks* and emirs of Iraq and elsewhere to notify them of these changes; and because of his having prepared the way during his father's lifetime by announcing his position to them all, they now believed his word, especially in Baghdad, where a decree was issued confirming his conversion to Islam, and all manner of favours were shown to him: a correspondence was opened with him and he was addressed with titles of honour ... He became known as Jalal al-Din the Neo-Muslim and during his reign his followers were called Neo-Muslims.' The psychologist may also note that while differing from his Ismaili father, Hasan seems to have been strongly attached to his devoutly Sunni mother.

The people of Qazvin, not unnaturally, expressed some doubts about the genuineness of this conversion on the part of their old neighbours and enemies, and Jalal al-Din Hasan was at great pains to convince them of his sincerity. He made direct approaches to the city notables, and induced them to send a delegation to Alamut, to inspect the library and remove the works of which they disapproved. These included treatises by Hasan-i Sabbah and by Jalal al-Din Hasan's own ancestors and predecessors. 'Jalal al-Din,' says Juvayni, 'ordered these works to be burnt in the very presence of those Qazvinis and at their prompting; and he uttered curses and maledictions against his forefathers and the authors of that propaganda. I have seen a letter in the hands of the notables and cadis of Qazvin, which had been dictated by Jalal al-Din Hasan and in which he spoke of his adoption of Islam, and acceptance of the rites of the Shari'a, and deliverance from the heresy and belief of his forefathers and ancestors. And Jalal al-Din had written a few words in his own handwriting upon the front of that letter and in mentioning his deliverance from their religion, when he came to the names of his fathers and ancestors, he added the curse: "May God fill their graves with fire!" '[21]

Jalal al-Din's mother went on the Pilgrimage in the year 609/1212–13, and was treated with great respect and deference in Baghdad. It was unfortunate that her visit to Mecca coincided with the murder of the Sharif's cousin. The Sharif, who greatly resembled his cousin, was sure that he himself was the intended victim, and that the murderer was an assassin sent against him by the Caliph. Full of anger, he attacked and looted the Iraqi pilgrims, and exacted a heavy fine from them, much of which was paid by the lady from Alamut. Despite this mishap, Jalal al-Din was able to maintain his Muslim alliances; he became very friendly with the ruler of Arran and Azerbayjan, exchanging gifts and help of various kinds, and joining forces against their common enemy the ruler of Western Iran. In this they were supported by the Caliph, to whom they had made a joint approach.

From the Caliph too came help of another kind. 'After residing for a year and a half in Iraq, Arran and Azerbayjan Jalal al-Din now returned to Alamut. During these journeyings and in the course of his residence in those countries his claim to be a Muslim had been more widely accepted and Muslims now mixed with him more freely. He asked the emirs of Gilan for the hands of their women in marriage.' The emirs were understandably reluctant either to accept or to refuse the proposals of so redoubtable a suitor, and compromised by making their consent conditional on the sanction of the Caliph. A messenger was promptly sent from Alamut to Baghdad, and the Caliph obliged with a letter authorizing the emirs to give their daughters to Jalal al-Din 'in accordance with the laws of Islam'. Armed with this decree, he took four Gilani princesses to wife; one of them had the privilege of bearing the next Imam.[22]

Jalal al-Din Hasan's religious, military and matrimonial adventures illustrate the remarkable strength of his position. By a decree no less sudden and sweeping than that which introduced the Resurrection, he abolished it and restored the rule of law – and was obeyed, in Quhistan and Syria as well as in Rudbar. In the course of his campaigns, he left Alamut, as none of his predecessors had done, and stayed away for a year and a half without mishap. Instead of despatching murderers to kill officers and divines, he sent armies to conquer provinces and cities, and by building mosques and bathhouses in the villages completed the transformation of his domain from a lair of assassins to a respectable kingdom, linked by ties of matrimonial alliance to his neighbours.

Like other territorial princes, Jalal al-Din made and changed alliances. At first he seems to have supported the Khorazmshah, and even had the bidding-prayer recited in Rudbar in his name. Then he transferred his allegiance to the Caliph, and helped him in various ways, including the removal by assassination of a rebel emir who had entered the service of the Khorazmshah, and of a Sharif in Mecca. Later, he was quick to recognize and ingratiate himself with a new and terrible power that was rising in the East. 'They [the Ismailis] said that when the World-Emperor Jenghiz Khan set out from Turkestan, before he came to the countries of Islam, Jalal al-Din had in secret sent couriers to him and written letters tendering his submission and allegiance. This was alleged by the Heretics and the truth is not clear, but this much is evident, that when the armies of the World-Conquering Emperor Jenghiz Khan entered the countries of Islam, the first ruler on this side of the Oxus to send ambassadors, and present his duty, and accept allegiance was Jalal al-Din.'²³

In November 1221, after a reign of only ten years, Jalal al-Din Hasan died. 'The disease of which Jalal al-Din died was dysentery and it was suspected that he had been poisoned by his wives in connivance with his sister and some of his kinsmen. The vizier, who by virtue of his will was administrator of the kingdom and tutor of his son Ala al-Din, put to death a great number of his relations, his sister, wives and intimates and confidants on this suspicion; and some he burnt.'²⁴

Jalal al-Din's restoration of the ritual laws and his accommodations with orthodoxy and the Caliphate have been variously interpreted. For Juvayni and other Persian Sunni historians, they were the expression of a genuine religious conversion – a desire to abandon the evil beliefs and ways of his predecessors, and bring his people back to the path of true Islam, from which they had strayed so far. The Caliph himself seems to have been satisfied with Hasan's good faith, and by intervening in support of his marriages in Gilan and giving a position of honour to the chief's mother on the pilgrimage, showed favour beyond the needs of the alliance. Even the doubters of Qazvin were persuaded of Jalal al-Din's sincerity. Joseph von Hammer, six centuries later in Metternich's Vienna, was less easily convinced and had his own little point to make. 'It is, therefore, more than probable, that Jelaleddin's conversion of the Ismailites to Islamism, so loudly proclaimed abroad, and his public abjuration of the doctrine of impiety, was nothing else than hypocrisy and deeply designed

policy, in order to re-establish the credit of the order, which had
been exposed to the anathemas of priests, and the ban of princes,
by the inconsiderate publication of their doctrines, and to gain
for himself the title of prince, instead of the dignity of grand-
master. Thus the Jesuits, when they were threatened with ex-
pulsion by the parliament, and with a bull of dissolution from the
Vatican – when, on all sides, the voices of cabinets and countries
rose against the principles of their morals and policy – denied
their doctrine of lawful rebellion and regicide, which had been
imprudently hinted at by some of their casuists, and openly
condemned the maxims which they, nevertheless, secretly
observed as the true rules of the order.'[25]

For the Ismailis too these changes required explanation. They
were after all not just a territorial principality subject to a local
chief, though this might be their aspect to the outside world;
still less were they a mere band of conspirators and murderers.
They were the faithful followers of a religion, with a proud
past and a cosmic mission – and like all true believers, they felt
the need to preserve the citadel of their integrity intact. This
required that all those changes – from the law to the Resurrection,
from the Resurrection to a show of Sunnism, and later back to
an Ismailism bound by law – be given a religious value and
significance.

An answer was found in two principles – in the doctrine of
Taqiyya, the concealment of one's true beliefs in the face of
danger, and in the old Ismaili concept of alternating periods
of occultation and manifestation. These corresponded to the
periods of outward law and inward truth, and were each in-
augurated by an imam bringing a new dispensation. 'The period of
each prophet of the outward forms of the holy law,' says an Ismaili
work of the thirteenth century, 'is called the period of occultation,
and the period of each *Qā'im*, who possesses the inner truths
of the laws of the Prophets, is called *qiyāma* (Resurrection).'[26]
A new period of occultation began in 1210, with the accession of Jalal al-Din Hasan. This time it was not the Imams
themselves that were hidden, as in the earlier periods of occultation, but the true nature of their mission. When the inner

truth was concealed, it did not matter greatly what outward form of legal observance was adopted.

On Jalal al-Din's death, he was succeeded by his only son, Ala al-Din Muhammad, a boy of nine. For some time Jalal al-Din's vizier was the effective ruler of Alamut, and seems to have maintained the policy of accommodation with the Sunni world. A reaction was, however, beginning to gather force. The observance of the holy law was no longer enforced in the Ismaili domains, and there are even reports that it was actively discouraged. Juvayni and the other Persian historians attribute these changes to the new Imam: 'Now Ala al-Din was but a child and had received no education, for according to their false creed ... their Imam is basically the same, whether an infant, a youth or an old man, and whatever he says or does ... must be right ... Accordingly, whatever course Ala al-Din might take no mortal could express disapproval thereof, and ... they would not allow him to be chastized, advised or guided aright ... the administration of affairs fell to the decision of women, and the foundations his father had laid were overthrown ... those who for fear of his father had adopted the Shari'a and Islam but in their foul hearts and murky minds still believed in the wicked creed of his grandfather ... seeing now no one to prevent and deter them from the commission of forbidden sins ... returned once more to their heresy ... and ... recovered their power ... And the rest, who had accepted Islam from conviction ... took fright ... and ... again concealed the fact that they were Muslims ...

'After this child had reigned for some five or six years ... he was overcome with the disease of melancholia ... No one dared contradict him ... all reports on affairs inside and outside his realm ... were kept hidden from him ... no adviser ever dared breathe a word ... to him ... Theft, highway robbery and assault were daily occurrences in his kingdom with and without his connivance; and he thought he could excuse such conduct with false words and the bestowal of money. And when these things had passed all bounds his life, wives, children, home, kingdom and wealth were forfeited to that madness and insanity.'[27]

Despite these difficulties, there were still capable leaders to direct the affairs of the sect, and the reign of Ala al-Din was a period of both intellectual and political activity. One of the recognized duties – and glories – of a Muslim ruler was the patronage of science and learning, and the Ismaili Imams had not been backward in this respect. The library of Alamut was famous – even the strongly hostile Juvayni admits to his interest in it – and at this period it attracted a number of scholars from outside. Foremost among these was the philosopher, theologian and astronomer Nasir al-Din Tusi (1201–74) who stayed there for a number of years. At this time he passed as an Ismaili, and indeed wrote Ismaili treatises which are still accepted as authoritative by the sect. Later he claimed to be a Twelver Shi'ite, whose association with the Ismailis had been involuntary. Which of his allegiances, if either, was *taqiyya* remains uncertain.

During the early years of Ala al-Din's reign, the situation in Iran was favourable to a further Ismaili expansion. The Khorazmian Empire had been shattered by the impact of Mongol invasion, and while the last of the Khorazmshahs, Sultan Jalal al-Din, was trying vainly to restore his broken kingdom, the Ismailis successfully extended their own. At about this time they seized the city of Damghan, near the fortress of Girdkuh, and apparently tried to capture Rayy, where in about 1222 the Khorazmians ordered a massacre of Ismaili da'is.

In 1227 Sultan Jalal al-Din forced the Ismailis to accept a truce, and to pay tribute to him for the city of Damghan. Shortly before this, a Khorazmian officer called Orkhan had been assassinated as a reprisal for raids against the Ismaili settlements in Quhistan. Nasawi, the biographer of the Khorazmshah Jalal al-Din, paints a lively picture of the scene: 'Three of the fida'is fell upon Orkhan and killed him outside the city. Then they entered the city with their daggers in their hands, shouting the name of Ala al-Din, until they reached the gate of [the vizier] Sharaf al-Mulk. They went into the secretariat building, but did not find him, since he was at that moment in the Sultan's palace. They wounded a servant and rushed out again, shouting their rallying-cry and vaunting their success. The common people threw stones at them from the roof-tops, until they battered them to death. With their last breaths they shouted: "We are sacrifices for our Lord Ala al-Din".'

It was at this time that Badr al-Din Ahmad, the envoy of Alamut, was on his way to see the Sultan. Hearing of these events he was not unnaturally somewhat apprehensive about his reception, and wrote to the vizier asking his advice on whether to continue his journey or turn back. The vizier, fearing for his own life, was only too happy to welcome the Ismaili envoy, hoping that his presence 'would safeguard him from the fearful fate and dreadful death that had befallen Orkhan'. He therefore urged the envoy to join him and promised to do all he could to help him in his mission.

The two now travelled together, the vizier making every effort to ingratiate himself with his redoubtable guest. Their friendship, however, was marred by an unfortunate incident. 'When they reached the plain of Serab, in a moment of abandon at a drinking session, when his potations had had their effect on him, Badr al-Din said: "Even here in your own army we have our fida'is, who are well established and pass as your own men – some in your stables, some in the service of the Sultan's chief pursuivant." Sharaf al-Mulk insisted on seeing them, and gave him his kerchief as a token of safe-conduct. Badr al-Din thereupon summoned five fida'is, and when they came one of them, an insolent Indian, said to Sharaf al-Mulk: "I would have been able to kill you on such and such a day at such and such a place; I did not do so because I had not yet received orders to deal with you." When Sharaf al-Mulk heard these words he cast off his cloak and sat before them in his shirt and said: "What is the cause of this? What does Ala al-Din want of me? For what sin or shortcomings on my part does he thirst for my blood? I am his slave as I am the Sultan's slave, and here I am before you. Do with me as you will!"' Word of this reached the Sultan, who was infuriated by Sharaf al-Mulk's abjectness and at once sent orders to him to burn the five fida'is alive. The vizier pleaded for mercy for them, but in vain, and was compelled to carry out the Sultan's orders. 'A great fire was kindled at the entrance to his tent, and the five men were thrown into it. As they were burning, they cried out: "We are sacrifices for our lord Ala al-Din!", until their souls left their bodies which were reduced to ashes and scattered by the winds.' As an added precaution, the Sultan executed the chief pursuivant, in punishment for his negligence.

Nasawi personally witnessed the aftermath. 'One day I was with Sharaf al-Mulk at Bardha'a, when an envoy called Salah al-Din came to him from Alamut and said: "You have burnt five of our fida'is. If you value your safety, you must pay a bloodwit of 10,000 dinars for each of them." These words appalled and terrified Sharaf al-Mulk, so that he became incapable of thought or action. He favoured the envoy above all others with generous gifts and splendid honours, and ordered me to write him an official letter, reducing by 10,000 dinars the annual tribute of 30,000 dinars which they were supposed to bring to the Sultan's treasury. Sharaf al-Mulk affixed his seal to the document.'[28]

The agreement between the Khorazmshah and the Ismailis did not prove very effective. Desultory quarrels with Sultan Jalal al-Din continued, while the Ismailis maintained friendly relations with the two main enemies of the Khorazmians – the Caliph in the West and the Mongols in the East. In 1228 the Ismaili diplomat Badr al-Din travelled east across the Oxus to the Mongol court; a westbound Ismaili caravan of seventy men was stopped and massacred by the Khorazmians, on the alleged grounds that a Mongol envoy to Anatolia was travelling with them. Bickering between the Ismailis and the Khorazmians continued for many years, enlivened from time to time by fighting, murder or negotiation.

On one occasion Nasawi was sent on an embassy to Alamut to demand the balance of the tribute that was owing for Damghan. He describes his mission with some satisfaction. 'Ala al-Din favoured me above all the other envoys of the Sultan, treating me with great respect and bounty. He dealt generously with me, and gave me twice the usual amount in gifts and robes of honour. He said: "This is an honourable man. Generosity to such a man is never wasted." The value of what was bestowed on me, in cash and in kind, was near to 3,000 dinars, including two robes

TRAICTE DE
L'ORIGINE DES
ANCIENS ASSASINS
PORTE-COVTEAVX.

Auec quelques exemples de leurs atten-
tats & homicides és perſonnes d'au-
cuns Roys, Princes, & Seigneurs de
la Chreſtienté.

Par M. DENIS LEBEY-DE BATILLY Con-
ſeiller du Roy, Maiſtre des Requeſtes de ſon hoſtel
& Couronne de Nauarre, & commis par ſa Maieſté
à l'exercice de l'Eſtat de Preſident en la ville de Metſ.

A LYON.

Par VINCENT VASPAZE.

M. DC III. 115

The title page of Lebey de Batilly's *Traicté de l'Origine des Anciens Assasins Porte-Couteaux*, published in Lyon, 1603.

ابر كاه باهره ٤ هم حي مي كرد وا وما قـا ردر دلىا اذر نحد حميد سد دحسن ببت لى غازان اولوا الـشــد رظام الملك

ابا غلبر ما استی كینه بود كـ قتل هذا الشيطان اولا التعادة نال ع اوزاز هنـاه وانـدكدشنه وسيداط رظام الملك وحال تاصدان اوجهان سنت آمد

The assassination of the Nizam al-Mulk. From a Persian manuscript of the *Jami al-tavarikh* of Rashid al-Din, in the library of the Topkapi Palace Museum, Istanbul (Treasury 1653). Early 14th century.

Authors, with scribe and attendants. From an Arabic manuscript of the *Rasa'il Ikhwan al-Safa* (Epistles of the Sincere Brethren—see p. 30 above), in the library of the Süleymaniye mosque, Istanbul. Completed A.D. 1287 (Esad Esendi 3638).

Hülegü on his way to capture the Ismaili castles in the year 654/1256.
From a Persian manuscript of the *Jami al-tavarikh*, in the library of the
Royal Asiatic Society of Bengal, Calcutta; ca. A.D. 1430.

Hülegü. From an album of drawings in the British Museum
(Ms. Add. 18803).

An inscription on the wall of the castle of Masyaf, in Syria. 13th century.

An aerial view of the massive Assassin castle of Qa'in.

A closer view of the walls of Qa'in.

The castle of Lamasar.

The rock of Alamut, with the castle on its crest.

The Assassin stronghold of Maymundiz.

View of the valley from Qal'a Bozi, near Isfahan.

The castle of Masyaf.

Entrance to the citadel of Aleppo.

of honour, each consisting of a satin cloak, a hood, a fur and a cape, one lined with satin and the other with Chinese crepe; two belts of 200 dinars weight; 70 pieces of cloth; two horses with saddles, bridles and harness and pommels; a thousand dinars in gold; four caparisoned horses; a string of Bactrian camels; and thirty robes of honour for my suite.'[29] Even allowing for some exaggeration, it is clear that the lord of Alamut was well provisioned with the good things of this world.

The quarrel with the Khorazmshah was not the only concern of the Ismailis. Nearer home, they came to blows with the rulers of Gilan, relations with whom can not have been improved by the summary execution of the Gilani princesses after the death of Jalal al-Din Hasan; at some time the Ismailis acquired some additional territory in Gilan, around Tarim. Relations with their old enemies in Qazvin, on the other hand, were fairly peaceful. Ala al-Din Muhammad, somewhat surprisingly, was the devoted disciple of a Shaykh in Qazvin, and sent him a yearly grant of 500 gold dinars, which the Shaykh spent on food and drink. When the Qazvinis reproached the Shaykh for living on the money of the heretics, he replied: 'The Imams hold it lawful to take the blood and money of the heretics; surely it is doubly lawful when they offer it of their own free will.' Ala al-Din told the people of Qazvin that it was only because of the Shaykh that he spared the city. 'Were he not there, I would bring the dust of Qazvin to the castle of Alamut in panniers.'[30]

Amid wars, raids, and assassinations, the Ismailis had not forgotten their primary purpose of preaching and conversion, and at about this time gained one of their most important successes in the implanting of their faith in India. The 'old preaching' of the Musta'lian Ismailis had been firmly established in India, especially on the Gujerati coast, for generations; a missionary from Iran now carried the Nizari 'new preaching' to the Indian subcontinent, which in later times became the main centre of their sect.

Juvayni and the other Persian Sunni historians paint a very hostile picture of Ala al-Din Muhammad, who appears as a drunken degenerate subject to fits of melancholia and madness.

During his last years he came into conflict with his eldest son Rukn al-Din Khurshah, whom he had designated, while still a child, as heir to the Imamate. Later he tried to revoke this nomination and appoint one of his other sons, but the Ismailis, 'in accordance with their tenets, refused to accept this and said that only the first designation was valid'.

The conflict between father and son came to a head in 1255. In this year 'Ala al-Din's insanity grew worse and ... his displeasure with Rukn al-Din increased ... Rukn al-Din felt that his life was not safe ... and on this account he was planning to flee from him, go to the castles in Syria and gain possession of them; or else to seize Alamut, Maymundiz and some of the [other] castles of Rudbar, which were full of treasure and stores and ... rise in rebellion ... Most of the ministers and chief men in Ala al-Din's kingdom had become apprehensive of him, for none was sure of his life.

'Rukn al-Din used the following argument as a decoy. "Because," he said, "of my father's evil behaviour the Mongol army intends to attack this kingdom, and my father is concerned about nothing. I shall secede from him and send messengers to the Emperor of the Face of the Earth [the Mongol Khan] and to the servants of his Court and accept submission and allegiance. And henceforth I shall allow no one in my kingdom to commit an evil act [and so ensure] that land and people may survive."'

In this predicament, the Ismaili leaders agreed to support Rukn al-Din, even against his father's men; their only reservation was that they would not raise their hands against Ala al-Din himself. The Imam, even when demented, was still sacrosanct, and to touch him would have been sacrilege as well as treason.

Fortunately for the Ismailis – or for all but a few of them – no such terrible choice was required. About a month after this agreement, Rukn al-Din was taken ill and lay helpless in bed. While he was thus visibly incapacitated, his father Ala al-Din, asleep, according to Juvayni, in a drunken stupor, was murdered by unknown assailants. This happened on 1 December 1255. The assassination of the assassin chief in his own stronghold gave rise to wild suspicions and accusations. Some of the dead Imam's retainers who had been seen near the site of the murder were put to death, and it was even claimed that a group of his closest associates had conspired against him and brought outsiders from Qazvin to Alamut to carry out the deed. Eventually, they agreed on a culprit: 'After a week had passed the clarity of the signs and indications caused it to be decided ... and unanimously agreed that Hasan of Mazandaran, who was Ala al-Din's chief favourite and his inseparable companion night and day and the repository of all his secrets, was the person who had killed him. It was said too that Hasan's wife, who was Ala al-Din's mistress and from whom Hasan had not concealed the facts of the murder, had revealed that secret to Rukn al-Din. Be that as it may, after a week had passed, Hasan was put to death, his body burnt and several of his children, two daughters and a son, likewise burnt; and Rukn al-Din reigned in his father's stead.'[31]

During the last years of Ala al-Din Muhammad's reign the Ismailis drew nearer to the final confrontation with the most terrible of all their enemies – the Mongols. By 1218 the armies of Jenghiz Khan, the ruler of the new Empire that had arisen in Eastern Asia, had reached the Jaxartes river, and become the immediate neighbours of the Khorazmshah. A border incident soon provided the pretext for a new advance westwards. In 1219 Jenghiz Khan led his armies across the Jaxartes into the lands of Islam. By 1220 he had captured the ancient Muslim cities of Samarqand and Bukhara and reached the Oxus river; in the following year he crossed the Oxus, captured Balkh, Marv and Nishapur, and made himself master of all eastern Iran. The death of the Khan in 1227 brought only a brief respite. In 1230 his successor launched a new attack on the faltering Khorazmian state; by 1240 the Mongols had overrun western Iran, and were invading Georgia, Armenia, and northern Mesopotamia.

The final attack came in the middle of the thirteenth century. The great Khan, now ruling from Peking, sent a new expedition under the command of the Mongol prince Hülegü, the grandson of Jenghiz Khan, with orders to subjugate all the Muslim lands as far as Egypt. Within a few months the long-haired Mongol horsemen thundered across Iran, carrying all before them, and in

January 1258 converged on the city of Baghdad. The last of the Caliphs, after a brief and futile attempt at resistance, begged in vain for quarter. The Mongol warriors stormed, looted and burned the city, and on 20 February the Caliph, with as many of his kin as could be found, was put to death. The house of Abbas, for half a millennium the titular heads of Sunni Islam, had ceased to reign.

The Imams of Alamut, like other Muslim rulers of the time, were by no means single-minded in opposition to the heathen Mongol invaders of Islam. The Caliph al-Nasir, locked in combat with the Khorazmshah, had not been displeased by the appearance of a new and dangerous enemy on the far side of the Khorazmian Empire – and his ally, the Imam Jalal al-Din Hasan, had been among the first to send messages of good will to the Khan. Sometimes, indeed, the Ismailis showed solidarity with their Sunni neighbours against this new menace. When Jenghiz Khan was conquering eastern Iran, the Ismaili chief in Quhistan gave a generous welcome to Sunni refugees in his mountain fastnesses. 'I found him,' says a Muslim visitor, speaking of the Ismaili chief in Quhistan, 'a person of infinite learning ... with wisdom, science, and philosophy, in such wise, that a philosopher and sage like unto him there was not in the territory of Khurasan. He used greatly to cherish poor strangers and travellers; and such Muslims of Khurasan as had come into proximity with him he was wont to take under his guardianship and protection. On this account his assemblies contained some of the most distinguished of the Ulema of Khurasan ... and he had treated all of them with honour and reverence, and showed them much kindness. They stated to this effect, that, during those first two or three years of anarchy in Khurasan, one thousand honorary dresses, and seven hundred horses, with trappings, had been received from his treasury and stables by Ulema and poor strangers.' His ability to do this suggests that the Ismaili centres were immune from attack, and his generosity soon brought a complaint to Alamut from his subjects, who requested – and obtained – a governor less lavish with Ismaili money to outsiders. The historian Minhaj-i Siraj Juzjani, in the service of the rulers of

Sistan, went on three visits to the Ismaili centres in Quhistan – on diplomatic missions concerned with reopening trade routes, and on a shopping expedition, to buy 'clothing and other requisites', which had become rare in eastern Iran 'in consequence of the irruption of the infidels'. Clearly, the Ismailis of Quhistan were turning their immunity to good advantage.

Whatever understanding may have existed between the Ismailis and the Mongols, it did not last. The new masters of Asia could not tolerate the continued independence of this dangerous and militant band of devotees – and there was no lack of pious Muslims among their friends and associates to remind them of the danger which the Ismailis presented. The chief Qadi of Qazvin, it is said, appeared before the Khan in a shirt of mail, and explained that he had to wear this at all times under his clothes, because of the ever-present danger of assassination.

The warning was not wasted. An Ismaili embassy to the grand assembly in Mongolia was turned away, and the Mongol general in Iran advised the Khan that his two most obstinate enemies were the Caliph and the Ismailis. At Karakorum precautions were taken to guard the Khan against attack by Ismaili emissaries. When Hülegü led his expedition into Iran in 1256, the Ismaili castles were his first objective.

Even before his arrival, the Mongol armies in Iran, with Muslim encouragement, had launched attacks on the Ismaili bases in Rudbar and Quhistan, but achieved only a limited success. An advance in Quhistan was repelled by an Ismaili counter-attack, while an assault on the great fortress of Girdkuh failed utterly. The Ismailis in their castles might well have been in a position to offer a sustained resistance to Mongol attacks – but the new Imam decided otherwise.

One of the questions on which Rukn al-Din Khurshah had disagreed with his father was that of resistance or collaboration with the Mongols. On his accession, he tried to make peace with his Muslim neighbours; 'acting contrary to his father's disposition he began to lay the foundations of friendship with those people. He likewise sent messengers to all his provinces ordering the people to behave as Muslims and keep the roads secure.' Having thus protected his position at home, he sent an envoy to Yasa'ur Noyan, the Mongol commander in Hamadan, with instructions to say that 'now that it was his turn to reign he would tread the path of submission and scrape the dust of disaffection from the countenance of loyalty'.[33]

Yasa'ur advised Rukn al-Din to go and make his submission in person to Hülegü, and the Ismaili Imam compromised by sending his brother Shahanshah. The Mongols made a premature attempt to move into Rudbar, but were driven back by Ismailis in fortified positions and withdrew after destroying the crops. In the meantime other Mongol forces had again invaded Quhistan, and captured several of the Ismaili centres.

A message now arrived from Hülegü, who professed his satisfaction with Shahanshah's embassy. Rukn al-Din himself had committed no crimes; if he would destroy his castles and come and submit in person, the Mongol armies would spare his territories. The Imam temporized. He dismantled some of his castles, but made only token demolitions at Alamut, Maymundiz and Lamasar, and asked for a year's grace before presenting himself in person. At the same time he sent orders to his governors in Girdkuh and Quhistan 'to present themselves before the king and give expression to their loyalty and submission'. This they did – but the castle of Girdkuh remained in Ismaili hands. A message from Hülegü to Rukn al-Din demanded that he attend on him immediately at Damavand. If he could not reach there within five days, he should send his son in advance.

Rukn al-Din sent his son – a boy of seven. Hülegü, perhaps suspecting that this was not really his son, sent him back on the grounds that he was too young, and suggested that Rukn al-Din send another of his brothers to relieve Shahanshah. Meanwhile the Mongols were drawing nearer to Rudbar, and when Rukn al-Din's embassy reached Hülegü, they found him only three days' march from Alamut. The Mongol's answer was an ultimatum: 'if Rukn al-Din destroyed the castle of Maymundiz and came to present himself in person before the King, he would, in accordance with His Majesty's gracious custom, be received with kindness and honour; but that if he failed to consider the consequences of his actions, God alone knew [what would then befall him].'³⁴ Meanwhile the Mongol armies were already entering Rudbar and taking up positions around the castles. Hülegü himself directed the siege of Maymundiz, in which Rukn al-Din was staying.

There seems to have been some difference of opinion among the Ismailis, between those who thought it wise to surrender and get the best terms they could from Hülegü, and those who preferred to fight to the end. Rukn al-Din himself was clearly of the first opinion, and was no doubt encouraged in this policy by advisers such as the astronomer Nasir al-Din Tusi, who hoped – with reason – that after the surrender he would be able to make his own accommodation with the Mongols and embark on a new career under their aegis. It was Tusi who, we are told, advised the Imam to surrender on the grounds that the stars were inauspicious – Tusi again who went on Rukn al-Din's final embassy from the fortress of Maymundiz to the camp of the besiegers, to negotiate the capitulation. Hülegü agreed to receive Rukn al-Din, his family and dependents and his treasure. As Juvayni puts it, 'he ... offered his treasures as a token of his allegiance. These were not so splendid as fame had reported them but, such as they were, they were brought out of the castle. The greater part thereof was distributed by the King among his troops.'³⁵

Rukn al-Din was well received by Hülegü, who even indulged his personal whims. An interest in Bactrian camels bought a gift of 100 females of the species. The gift was insufficient; Rukn al-Din was interested in camel-fighting, and could not wait for them to breed. He therefore indented for 30 he-camels. A still more striking benefaction was permission to marry a Mongol girl with whom he fell in love and for whom he declared his willingness, not wholly figuratively, to give up his kingdom.³⁶

Hülegü's interest in Rukn al-Din was obvious. The Ismailis still held some castles, and could give a lot of trouble. The Ismaili Imam, urging them to surrender, was a valuable addition to the Mongol court. His family, household and servants, with his personal effects and animals, were billeted in Qazvin (the comments of the Qazvinis are not recorded), and he himself accompanied Hülegü on his further expeditions.

Rukn al-Din earned his keep. On his instructions, most of the fortresses in Rudbar, near Girdkuh, and in Quhistan, surrendered, thus saving the Mongols the immense cost and uncertain fortunes of siege and assault. Their number is put at about a hundred – certainly an exaggeration. In two places the commandants refused to surrender, disregarding the orders of their own Imam – perhaps in the belief that he was acting in *taqiyya*, under duress. These two were the great Rudbar strongholds of Alamut and Lamasar. Mongol armies invested both fortresses, and after a few days the commandant of Alamut changed his mind. 'The garrison, having cast a glance at the consequences of the matter and the vagaries of Fate, sent a messenger to sue for quarter and beg for favourable treatment. Rukn al-Din intervened on their behalf and the King was pleased to pass over their crimes. And at the end of Dhu'l-Qa'da of that year [beginning of December 1256] all the inmates of that seminary of iniquity and nest of Satan came down with all their goods and belongings. Three days later the army climbed up to the castle and seized whatever those people had been unable to carry off. They quickly set fire to the various buildings and with the broom of destruction cast the dust thereof to the winds, levelling them with their foundations.'[37] Lamasar held out for another year, and finally submitted to the Mongols in 1258. In Girdkuh, the Ismailis, rejecting Rukn al-Din's orders, were able to retain control of the fortress, and were not finally overcome until 1270.

The surrender of most of the castles made Rukn al-Din unnecessary to the Mongols; the resistance of Lamasar and Girdkuh showed that he was useless. Orders were sent to the Mongol officers in Qazvin to kill the Imam's family and attendants; he himself, at his own request, went on the long journey to the Mongol capital at Karakorum, where the Khan refused to receive him. 'There was no need to bring him on so long a journey,' said the Khan, 'for our laws are well-known.' Let Rukn al-Din return, and see that the remaining castles were surrendered and dismantled; then he might be permitted to make obeisance. In fact he was not given the opportunity. On the edge of the Khangay range, on the way back to Persia, he was led away from the road, on the pretext of going to a feast, and was murdered. 'He and his followers were kicked to a pulp and then put to the sword; and of him and his stock no trace was left, and he and his kindred became but a tale on men's lips and a tradition in the world.'[38]

The extirpation of the Ismailis in Persia was not quite as thorough as Juvayni suggests. In the eyes of the sectaries, Rukn al-Din's small son succeeded him as Imam on his death, and lived to sire a line of Imams from which, in due course, the Aga Khans emerged in the nineteenth century. For a while the Ismailis remained active, and in 1275 were even able briefly to recapture Alamut. Their cause was however lost, and from this time onwards they survived only as a minor sect in the Persian-speaking lands, scattered through eastern Persia, Afghanistan, and what is now Soviet Central Asia. In Rudbar they have disappeared entirely.

The destruction of Alamut, and the final humbling of Ismaili power, are vividly depicted by Juvayni. 'In that breeding-ground of heresy in the Rudbar of Alamut the home of the wicked adherents of Hasan-i Sabbah . . . there remains not one stone of the foundations upon another. And in that flourishing abode of innovation the Artist of Eternity Past wrote with the pen of violence upon the portico of each one['s dwelling] the verse: "These their empty houses are empty ruins" [Qur'an, xxvii, 53]. And in the market-place of those wretches' kingdom the muezzin Destiny has uttered the cry of "Away then with the wicked people!" [Qur'an, xxiii, 43]. Their luckless womenfolk, like their empty religion, have been utterly destroyed. And the gold of those crazy, double-dealing counterfeiters which appeared to be unalloyed has proved to be base lead.

'Today, thanks to the glorious fortune of the World-Illuminating King, if an assassin still lingers in a corner he plies a woman's trade; wherever there is a da'i there is an announcer of death; and every *rafiq* has become a thrall. The propagators of Ismailism have fallen victims to the swordsmen of Islam. . . . The kings of the Greeks and Franks, who turned pale for fear of these accursed ones, and paid them tribute, and were not ashamed of that ignominy, now enjoy sweet slumber. And all the inhabitants of the world, and in particular the Faithful, have been relieved of their evil machinations and unclean beliefs. Nay, the whole of mankind, high and low, noble and base, share in this rejoicing. And compared with these histories that of Rustam the son of Dastan has become but an ancient fable.'39

'So was the world cleansed which had been polluted by their evil. Wayfarers now ply to and fro without fear or dread or the inconvenience of paying a toll and pray for the [continued] fortune of the happy King who uprooted their foundations and left no trace of any one of them. And in truth that act was the balm of Muslim wounds and the cure to the disorders of the Faith. Let those who shall come after this age and era know the extent of the mischief they wrought and the confusion they cast into the hearts of men. Such as were on terms of agreement with them, whether kings of former times or contemporary rulers, went in fear and trembling [for their lives] and [such as were] hostile to them were day and night in the straits of prison for dread of their scoundrelly minions. It was a cup that had been filled to overflowing; it seemed as a wind that had died. "This is a warning for those who reflect," [Qur'an, vi, 116], and may God do likewise unto all tyrants!'40

5

The Old Man of the Mountain

While Hasan-i Sabbah was still ruling in the castle of Alamut, and the words and weapons of his emissaries were bringing his message to the people and princes of Iran, a few of his followers set out on a long and hazardous journey, through enemy country, to the West. Their destination was Syria; their purpose to take the New Preaching to the old Ismailis in that country, and to extend the war against the Seljuq power, which had recently enveloped all the lands from Asia Minor to the borders of Egypt.

The New Preaching had arisen in Iran, and its exponents had won their first great success in lands of Iranian speech and culture – in western and eastern Persia, and in Central Asia. For their first attempt at expansion to the West, Syria was an obvious choice, Iraq, immediately to the west of Persia, held few opportunities. No doubt there were Ismaili sympathizers in the Iraqi cities, but the flat river valleys offered little scope for the Ismaili strategy of penetration, entrenchment and attack. Syria, however, was a different matter. Between Taurus and Sinai, a broken landscape of mountains and valleys and deserts sheltered a population of great diversity, with strong local traditions of independence. Unlike the neighbouring river-valley societies of Iraq and Egypt, Syria had rarely known political unity. The pattern was one of fragmentation – of sectarian and regional particularism, and of recurring conflict and change. Though their common speech was Arabic, the Syrians were divided into many faiths and sects, including several with extremist Shi'ite beliefs. The first Shi'ite pretender had appeared in Syria in the eighth century; by the end of the ninth and the beginning of the tenth century the hidden Imams of the Ismailis could count on sufficient local support to make Syria the seat of their secret headquarters and the scene of their first bid for power. The establishment of the Fatimid Caliphate in Egypt, and its expansion into Asia, brought Syria under intermittent Ismaili rule in the late tenth and eleventh centuries, and opened the country to Ismaili propaganda and instruction.

Besides the overt Ismailis, there were other sects near enough to Ismailism in doctrine and outlook to make them a promising recruiting ground for the emissaries from Alamut. Such for example were the Druzes of Mount Lebanon and the adjoining areas, a dissident Ismaili sect which had only recently broken away from the main body, and had not yet fallen into the ossified exclusiveness of later times. Another group of potential supporters was the Nusayris, also called Alawis, Twelver Shi'ite in origin, but much affected by extremist ideas. These were established in the hill country east and north-east of Lattakia, and perhaps also, at that date, in Tiberias and the Jordan valley.

The time, as well as the place, was propitious. The first Turcoman bands are reported to have entered Syria in 1064. During the seventies of the eleventh century first Turkish free-booters, and then regular Seljuq armies invaded the country, and soon the whole of Syria, apart from a coastal strip retained by the Fatimids, was under Seljuq rule or suzerainty. The overlord was Tutush, the brother of the Great Sultan Malikshah.

In 1095 Tutush was killed in battle in Persia in the course of a fraternal struggle for the supreme Sultanate. The Syrian pattern of regional fragmentation and the Seljuq tradition of dynastic dispute combined to shatter his kingdom in pieces. Syria was again split into small states, now ruled by Seljuq princes and officers; the most important were Tutush's sons Ridwan and Duqaq, who held the rival cities of Aleppo and Damascus.

It was at this moment of disarray and mounting conflict that a new force entered the country – the Crusaders. Coming through Antioch in the North, they advanced swiftly down the Syrian coast, where there was no power capable of resisting them, and established four Latin states based on Edessa, Antioch, Tripoli and Jerusalem.

The extension of Seljuq power to Syria brought with it many of the problems of social change and tension already familiar in the East. The shock of Latin invasion and conquest can only have added to the distress and discouragement of the Syrians, and made them more ready to welcome the bearers of a message of messianic hope – especially those whose existing beliefs prepared them for the acceptance of such a message. The Fatimids of Cairo still had followers in Syria, who held to the Old Preaching of Ismailism – but the ignominious weakness of the Cairo régime, and its failure to resist either the Turkish or the Latin menace, must have led many to transfer their allegiance to the more active, more militant and, so it seemed, more successful branch. Some of the Shi'ites and most of the Sunnis seem to have remained faithful to their old loyalties; but there were many who rallied to the new force, which alone seemed to offer an effective challenge to the invaders and rulers of the country.

From the start, the agents of Alamut in Syria tried to use the same methods and achieve the same results as their comrades in Persia. Their aim was to seize or otherwise acquire fortresses, for use as bases in a campaign of terror. To this end, they tried to invoke and direct the zeal of the faithful, especially in mountain areas; at the same time, they did not disdain the discreet co-operation of princes, where a limited and temporary alliance seemed expedient to both sides.

Despite such help, and despite occasional successes, the Ismailis found their task in Syria much harder than it had been in Persia – perhaps in part because they were Persians, working in an alien surrounding. Almost half a century of determined effort was needed before they were able to attain their first objective, and consolidate a group of strongholds in central Syria, in the mountain area known then as the Jabal Bahra', and today as the Jabal Ansariyya. Their leaders, as far as they are known, were all Persians, sent from Alamut and acting under the orders of Hasan-i Sabbah and his successors. Their struggle to establish themselves falls into three main phases. During the first two phases, ending in 1113 and 1130, they operated successively from Aleppo and Damascus, with the connivance of the rulers of those cities, and tried to establish themselves in adjoining areas. Both ended in failure and disaster. During the third, which began in 1131, they were at last able to gain and fortify the bases which they needed.

The history of the Syrian Ismailis, as recorded by the Syrian historians, is chiefly the history of the assassinations which they perpetrated. The story begins on 1 May 1103, with the sensational murder of Janah al-Dawla, the ruler of Homs, in the cathedral mosque of the city during the Friday prayer. His assailants were Persians, disguised as Sufis, and they fell upon him on a signal from a shaykh who accompanied them. In the melée several of Janah al-Dawla's officers were killed; so too were the murderers. Significantly, most of the Turks in Homs fled to Damascus.

Janah al-Dawla was an enemy of Ridwan, the Seljuq ruler of Aleppo, and most of the chroniclers agree that Ridwan was implicated in the murder. Some gave further details. The leader of the Hashishiyya or Assassins, to use the name by which they were called in Syria, was a personage known as al-Hakim al-Munajjim, 'the physician-astrologer'. He and his friends had come from Persia and settled in Aleppo, where Ridwan had allowed them to practice and propagate their religion, and to use the city as a base for further activities. Aleppo had obvious advantages for the Assassins. The city had an important Twelver Shi'ite population, and was conveniently near the extremist Shi'a areas in the Jabal al-Summaq and the Jabal Bahra'. For Ridwan, a man of notoriously lax religious loyalties, the Assassins offered the possibility of mobilizing new elements of support, and compensating for his military weakness among his rivals in Syria.

The 'physician-astrologer' survived Janah al-Dawla only by two or three weeks, and was then succeeded as leader of the Assassins by another Persian, Abu Tahir al-Sa'igh, the goldsmith. Abu Tahir retained the favour of Ridwan and the freedom of Aleppo, and now made a series of attempts to seize strategic points in the mountains south of the city. He seems to have been

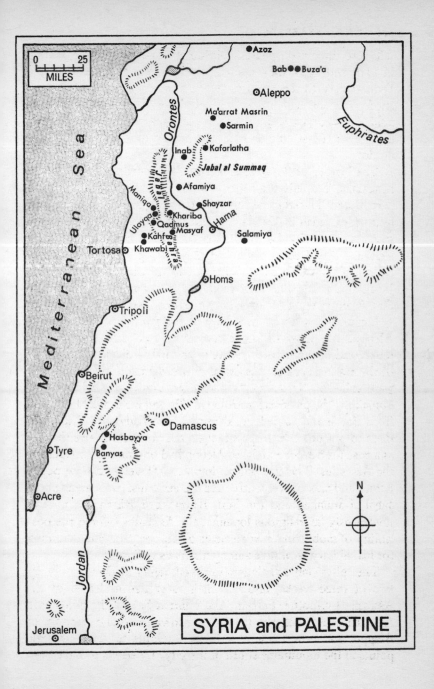

SYRIA and PALESTINE

able to call on local assistance, and may even have held some localities, though only for a short time.

The first documented attack was made in 1106, against Afamiya. Its ruler, Khalaf ibn Mula'ib, was a Shi'ite, probably an Ismaili – but of the Cairo, not the Alamut allegiance. In 1096 he had seized Afamiya from Ridwan, and demonstrated the suitability of the place by using it as a base for successful and wide-ranging brigandage. The Assassins decided that Afamiya would meet their needs very well, and Abu Tahir devised a plan to kill Khalaf and seize his citadel. Some of the inhabitants of Afamiya were local Ismailis, and through their leader Abu'l-Fath, a judge from near-by Sarmin, were privy to the plot. A group of six Assassins came from Aleppo to carry out the attack. 'They got hold of a Frankish horse, mule and accoutrements, with a shield and armour, and came with them ... from Aleppo to Afamiya, and said to Khalaf ... "We have come here to enter your service. We found a Frankish knight and killed him, and we have brought you his horse and mule and accoutrements." Khalaf gave them an honourable welcome, and installed them in the citadel of Afamiya, in a house adjoining the wall. They bored a hole through the wall and made a tryst with the Afamians ... who came in through the hole. And they killed Khalaf and seized the citadel of Afamiya.'[1] This was on 3 February 1106. Soon after, Abu Tahir himself arrived from Aleppo to take charge.

The attack on Afamiya, despite its promising start, did not succeed. Tancred, the crusading prince of Antioch, was in the neighbourhood, and took the opportunity to attack Afamiya. He seems to have been well informed of the situation, and brought with him, as a prisoner, a brother of Abu'l-Fath of Sarmin. At first he was content to levy tribute from the Assassins and leave them in possession, but in September of the same year he returned and blockaded the town into surrender. Abu'l-Fath of Sarmin was captured and put to death by torture; Abu Tahir and his companions were taken prisoner, and allowed to ransom themselves and return to Aleppo.

This first encounter of the Assassins with the Crusaders, and the frustration of their carefully laid plan by a crusading prince, does not seem to have led to any diversion of Assassin attention from Muslim to Christian objectives. Their main struggle was still against the masters, not the enemies of Islam. Their immediate aim was to seize a base, from whatever owners; their larger purpose was to strike at the Seljuq power, wherever it might appear.

In 1113 they achieved their most ambitious coup to date – the murder in Damascus of Mawdud, the Seljuq emir of Mosul, commander of an eastern expeditionary force that had come to Syria ostensibly to help the Syrian Muslims in their fight against the Crusaders. To the Assassins, such an expedition represented an obvious danger. They were not alone in their fears. In 1111, when Mawdud and his army reached Aleppo, Ridwan had closed the gates of the city against them, and the Assassins had rallied to his support. Contemporary gossip, as recorded by both Christian and Muslim sources, suggests that the murder of Mawdud was encouraged by the Muslim regent of Damascus.

The danger to the Assassins of eastern Seljuq influence became clear after the death of their patron Ridwan on 10 December 1113. Assassin activities in Aleppo had made them increasingly unpopular with the townspeople, and in 1111 an unsuccessful attempt on the life of a Persian from the East, a man of wealth and an avowed anti-Ismaili, had led to a popular outburst against them. After Ridwan's death, his son Alp Arslan at first followed his father's policy, and even ceded them a castle on the road to Baghdad. But a reaction soon came. A letter from the Seljuq Great Sultan Muhammad to Alp Arslan warned him against the Ismaili menace and urged him to destroy them. In the city, Ibn Badi', the leader of the townsfolk and commander of the militia, took the initiative, and persuaded the ruler to sanction strong measures. 'He arrested Abu Tahir the goldsmith and killed him, and he killed Isma'il the da'i, and the brother of the physician-astrologer, and the leaders of this sect in Aleppo. He arrested about 200 of them, and imprisoned some of them and confiscated their property. Some were interceded for, some released, some thrown from the top of the citadel, some killed. Some of them escaped, and scattered throughout the land.'[2]

Despite this setback, and their failure to secure a permanent castle-stronghold so far, the Persian Ismaili mission had not done too badly during the tenure of office of Abu Tahir. They had made contacts with local sympathizers, winning to the Assassin allegiance Ismailis of other branches and extremist Shi'ites of the various local Syrian sects. They could count on important local support in the Jabal al-Summaq, the Jazr, and the Banu Ulaym country – that is, in the strategically significant territory between Shayzar and Sarmin. They had formed nuclei of support in other places in Syria, and especially along their line of communication eastwards to Alamut. The Euphrates districts east of Aleppo were known as centres of extremist Shi'ism in both earlier and later periods, and although there is no direct evidence for these years, one may be certain that Abu Tahir did not neglect his opportunities. It is remarkable that as early as the spring of 1114 a force of about a hundred Ismailis from Afamiya, Sarmin and other places was able to seize the Muslim stronghold of Shayzar by a surprise attack, while its lord and his henchmen were away, watching the Easter festivities of the Christians. The attackers were defeated and destroyed by a counter-attack immediately after.

Even in Aleppo, despite the debacle of 1113, the Assassins were able to retain some foothold. In 1119 their enemy Ibn Badi' was expelled from the city, and fled to Mardin; the Assassins were waiting for him at the Euphrates crossing, and killed him together with his two sons. In the following year they demanded a castle from the ruler who, unwilling to cede it and afraid to refuse, resorted to the subterfuge of having it hastily demolished and then pretending to have ordered this just previously. The officer who conducted the demolition was assassinated a few years later. The end of Ismaili influence in Aleppo came in 1124, when the new ruler of the city arrested the local agent of the chief da'i and expelled his followers, who sold their property and departed.

It was a local agent, not the chief da'i himself, who by this time headed the Ismailis in Aleppo. After the execution of Abu Tahir, his successor, Bahram, transferred the main activities of the sect to the South, and was soon playing an active part in the affairs of Damascus. Like his predecessors, Bahram was a Persian, the nephew of al-Asadabadi, who had been executed in Baghdad in 1101. For a while 'he lived in extreme concealment and secrecy, and continually disguised himself, so that he moved from city to city and castle to castle without anyone being aware of his identity'.[3] He almost certainly had a hand in the murder of Bursuqi, the governor of Mosul, in the cathedral mosque of that city on 26 November 1126. Some at least of the eight assassins who, disguised as ascetics, fell upon him and stabbed him were Syrians. The Aleppine historian Kamal al-Din Ibn al-Adim tells a curious story. 'All those who attacked him were killed except for one youth, who came from Kafr Nasih, in the district of Azaz [north of Aleppo] and escaped unhurt. He had an aged mother, and when she heard that Bursuqi was killed and that those who attacked him were killed, knowing that her son was one of them, she rejoiced, and anointed her eyelids with kohl, and was full of joy; then after a few days her son returned unharmed, and she was grieved, and tore her hair and blackened her face.'[4]

From the same year, 1126, come the first definite reports of co-operation between the Assassins and the Turkish ruler of Damascus, Tughtigin. In January, according to the Damascene chronicler Ibn al-Qalanisi, Ismaili bands from Homs and elsewhere, 'noted for courage and gallantry', joined the troops of Tughtigin in an unsuccessful attack on the Crusaders. Towards the end of the year Bahram appeared openly in Damascus, with a letter of recommendation from Il-Ghazi, the new ruler of Aleppo. He was well received in Damascus, and with official protection soon acquired a position of power. His first demand, in accordance with the accepted strategy of the sect, was for a castle; Tughtigin ceded him the fortress of Banyas, on the border with the Latin kingdom of Jerusalem. But that was not all. Even in Damascus itself the Assassins were given a building, variously described as a 'palace' and a 'mission-house', which served them as headquarters. The Damascus chronicler puts the main blame for those events on the vizier al-Mazdagani, who, though not himself an Ismaili, was a willing accomplice in their plans and the evil influence behind the throne. Tughtigin, according to this view, disapproved of the Assassins, but tolerated them for tactical reasons, until the time came to strike a decisive blow against them. Other historians, while recognizing the role of the vizier, place the blame squarely on the ruler, and ascribe his action in large measure to the influence of Il-Ghazi, with whom Bahram had established friendly relations while still in Aleppo.

In Banyas, Bahram rebuilt and fortified the castle, and embarked on a course of military and propagandist action in the surrounding country. 'In all directions,' says Ibn al-Qalanisi, 'he dispatched his missionaries, who enticed a great multitude of the ignorant folk of the provinces and foolish peasantry from the villages and the rabble and scum. . . .'⁵ From Banyas, Bahram and his followers raided extensively, and may have captured some other places. But they soon came to grief. The Wadi al-Taym, in the region of Hasbayya, was inhabited by a mixed population of Druzes, Nusayris, and other heretics, who seemed to offer a favourable terrain for Assassin expansion. Baraq ibn Jandal, one of the chiefs of the area, was captured and put to death by treachery, and shortly afterwards Bahram and his forces set out to occupy the Wadi. There they encountered vigorous resistance from Dahhak ibn Jandal, the dead man's brother and sworn avenger. In a sharp engagement the Assassins were defeated and Bahram himself was killed.

Bahram was succeeded in the command of Banyas by another Persian, Isma'il, who carried on his policies and activities. The vizier al-Mazdagani continued his support. But soon the end came. The death of Tughtigin in 1128 was followed by an anti-Ismaili reaction similar to that which had followed the death of Ridwan in Aleppo. Here too the initiative came from the prefect of the city, Mufarrij ibn al-Hasan ibn al-Sufi, a zealous opponent of the sectaries and an enemy of the vizier. Spurred on by the prefect, as well as by the military governor Yusuf ibn Firuz, Buri, the son and heir of Tughtigin, prepared the blow. On Wednesday, 4 September 1129, he struck. The vizier was murdered by his orders at the levée, and his head cut off and publicly exposed. As the news spread, the town militia and the mob turned on the Assassins, killing and pillaging. 'By the next morning the quarters and streets of the city were cleared of the Batinites [= Ismailis] and the dogs were yelping and quarrelling over their limbs and corpses.'6 The number of Assassins killed in this outbreak is put at 6,000 by one chronicler, 10,000 by another and 20,000 by a third. In Banyas, Isma'il, realizing that his position was untenable, surrendered the fortress to the Franks and fled to the Frankish territories. He died at the beginning of 1130. The oft-repeated story of a plot by the vizier and the Assassins to surrender Damascus to the Franks rests on a single not very reliable source, and may be dismissed as an invention of hostile gossip.

Buri and his coadjutors took elaborate precautions to protect themselves against the vengeance of the Assassins, wearing armour and surrounding themselves with heavily armed guards; but without avail. The Syrian mission seems to have been temporarily disorganized, and it was from the centre of the sect in Alamut that the blow was struck. On 7 May 1131, two Persians, who, disguised as Turkish soldiers, had entered the service of Buri, struck him down. They are named in the roll of honour of Alamut.7 The assassins were at once hacked to pieces by the guards, but Buri himself died of his wounds in the following year. Despite this successful coup the Assassins never recovered their position in Damascus, and indeed, in so rigidly orthodox a city, can have had but little hope of doing so.

During this period the Assassins were fighting another enemy besides the Turks. In their eyes, the Fatimid Caliph who still reigned in Cairo was a usurper; it was a sacred duty to oust him and establish the Imamate of the line of Nizar. During the first half of the twelfth century more than one pro-Nizari revolt broke out and was suppressed in Egypt, and the government in Cairo devoted much attention to countering Nizari propaganda among their subjects. The caliph al-Amir issued a special rescript defending the claims of his own line to the succession and refuting the Nizari case. In an interesting appendix to this document the story is told how, when the Fatimid emissary read it to the Assassins of Damascus, it caused an uproar and so impressed one of them that he forwarded it to his chief, who added a refutation in the blank space at the end. The Nizari read this refutation to a meeting of Fatimid supporters in Damascus. The

Cairo emissary asked the caliph's aid in answering it, and received a further statement of the Musta'lian arguments. These events may be connected with the murder by an Assassin in Damascus in 1120 of a man alleged to have been spying on the Assassins for the Fatimid government.

The Assassins also used stronger and more characteristic arguments against their Fatimid rivals. In 1121 al-Afdal, the Commander of the Armies in Egypt, and the man primarily responsible for the dispossession of Nizar, was murdered by three Assassins from Aleppo; in 1130 the Caliph al-Amir himself was struck down by ten Assassins in Cairo. His hatred of the Nizaris was well-known, and it is related that after the death of Bahram, the latter's head, hands, and ring were taken by a native of the Wadi al-Taym to Cairo, where the bearer received rewards and a robe of honour.

Little is known of Assassin relations with the Franks in this period. Stories in later Muslim sources of Ismaili collaboration with the enemy are probably a reflection of the mentality of a later age, when the holy war for Islam filled the minds of most Near Eastern Muslims. At this time, the most that can be said is that the Assassins shared the general indifference of Muslim Syria to religious divisions. No Frankish victims to the daggers of the fida'is are known, but on at least two occasions Assassin forces came into conflict with the crusading armies. On the other hand, Assassin refugees from both Aleppo and Banyas sought refuge in Frankish lands. The surrender of Banyas to Frankish rather than Muslim rulers, when it had to be abandoned, was in all probability merely a matter of geography.

The next twenty years are taken up with the third, and successful, attempt of the Assassins to secure fortress-bases in Syria, this time in the Jabal Bahra', just to the south-west of the scene of their first endeavour in the Jabal al-Summaq. Their establishment followed an unsuccessful attempt by the Franks to win control of the area. In 1132–33 the Muslim lord of al-Kahf sold the mountain fortress of Qadmus, recovered from the Franks in the previous year, to the Assassins. A few years later his son ceded them al-Kahf itself in the course of a struggle with his cousins for the succession. In 1136-7 the Frankish garrison in Khariba was driven out by a group of Assassins, who succeeded in regaining control after being temporarily dislodged by the governor of Hama. Masyaf, the most important of the Assassin strongholds, was captured in 1140-1 from a governor appointed by the Banu Munqidh, who had purchased the castle in 1127-8. The other Assassin castles of Khawabi, Rusafa, Qulay'a, and Maniqa were all probably acquired about the same period, though little is known of the date or manner of their acquisition.

During this period of quiet consolidation, the Assassins made little impression on the outside world, and in consequence little is heard of them in the chronicles. Very few of their names are known. The purchaser of Qadmus is named as Abu'l-Fath, the last chief da'i before Sinan as Abu Muhammad. A Kurdish Assassin leader called Ali ibn Wafa' co-operated with Raymond of Antioch in his campaign against Nur al-Din, and perished with him on the battlefield in Inab in 1149. Only two assassinations are recorded in these years. In 1149 Dahhak ibn Jandal, the chief of the Wadi al-Taym, suffered the vengeance of the Assassins for his successful resistance to Bahram in 1128. A year or two later they murdered Count Raymond II of Tripoli at the gates of that city – their first Frankish victim.

Of the general policy of the Assassins in these years only the broadest outlines can be seen. To Zangi, the lord of Mosul, and his house they could feel only hostility. The rulers of Mosul had always been among the most powerful of the Turkish princes. Dominating the lines of communication between Syria and Persia, and in friendly relations with the Seljuqid rulers of the East, they offered a constant threat to the position of the Assassins, which was aggravated by their recurrent tendency to spread into Syria. Mawdud and Bursuqi had already been assassinated. The Zangids were more than once threatened. When they occupied Aleppo in 1128, the danger which they offered to the Ismailis became more direct. In 1148 Nur al-Din ibn Zangi abolished the Shi'ite formulae used hitherto in the call to prayer in Aleppo. This step, which aroused intense but ineffectual resentment among the Ismailis and other Shi'ites in the city, amounted to an open declaration of war against the heretics. In the circumstances it is not surprising to find an Assassin contingent fighting beside Raymond of Antioch, the only leader in Syria at the time who could offer effective resistance to the Zangids.

Meanwhile the greatest of all the Assassin chiefs of Syria had taken command. Sinan ibn Salman ibn Muhammad, known as Rashid al-Din, was a native of Aqr al-Sudan, a village near Basra, on the road to Wasit. He is variously described as an alchemist, a schoolmaster, and, on his own authority, as the son of one of the leading citizens of Basra. A contemporary Syrian writer describes a visit to Sinan and a conversation with him, in the course of which Sinan described his early career, his training, and the circumstances of his mission to Syria. 'I was brought up in Basra and my father was one of its notables. This doctrine entered into my heart. Then something occurred between me and my brothers which obliged me to leave them, and I went forth without provision or a mount. I made my way until I reached Alamut and entered it. Its ruler was Kiya Muhammad, and he had two sons called Hasan and Husayn. He put me in school with them and gave me exactly the same treatment as he gave them, in those things that are needful for the support, education, and clothing of children. I remained there until Kiya Muhammad died, and was succeeded by his son Hasan. He ordered me to go to Syria. I set forth as I had set forth from Basra, and only rarely did I approach any town. He had given me orders and letters. I entered Mosul and halted at the mosque of the carpenters and stayed the night there, and then I went on, not entering any town, until I reached Raqqa. I had a letter to one of our companions there. I delivered it to him, and he gave me provisions and hired me a mount as far as Aleppo. There I met another companion and delivered him another letter, and he too hired me a mount and sent me on to Kahf. My orders were to stay in this fortress, and I stayed there until Shaykh Abu Muhammad, the head of the Mission, died in the mountain. He was succeeded by Khwaja Ali b. Mas'ud, without appointment [from Alamut] but with the agreement of some of the company. Then the chief Abu Mansur, the nephew of Shaykh Abu Muhammad, and the chief Fahd conspired and sent someone to stab him to death as he was leaving his bath. The leadership remained consultative among them, and the murderers were arrested and imprisoned. Then the command came from Alamut to execute the murderer and release the chief Fahd. With it came a message, and an order to read it out to the company.'8 The main points of this narrative are confirmed by other sources, and amplified by the legendary biography of Sinan, which gives his period of waiting at Kahf as seven years. Sinan, clearly, was a protégé of Hasan ala dhikrihi-'l-salam, and the year when he revealed himself to the faithful in Syria was 1162, the year of Hasan's accession in Alamut. The story of the disputed succession may be a reflection of the disagreement between Hasan and his father.

In August 1164 Hasan proclaimed the Resurrection in Alamut, and sent messengers carrying the tidings to the Ismailis in other parts. It fell to Sinan to inaugurate the new dispensation in Syria. There is a curious contrast between the recording of these events in Persia and in Syria. In Persia the coming of the Resurrection was faithfully recorded by the Ismailis – and seems to have passed unnoticed among contemporary Sunnis; in Syria on the other hand the Ismailis seem to have forgotten it – while the Sunni historians, with appropriate relish and horror, repeat the rumours that reached them of the end of the law. 'I have heard,' says a contemporary 'that he [Sinan] allowed them to defile their mothers and sisters and daughters and released them from the fast of the month of Ramadan.'9

While this and similar reports are no doubt exaggerated, it is clear that the end of the law was proclaimed in Syria, and led to some excesses, which were finally stopped by Sinan himself. 'In the year 572 [1176–77],' says Kamal al-Din, 'the people of the Jabal al-Summaq gave way to iniquity and debauchery, and called themselves "the Pure". Men and women mingled in drinking sessions, no man abstained from his sister or daughter, the women wore men's clothes, and one of them declared that Sinan was his God.'10 The ruler of Aleppo sent an army against them, and they took to the mountains, where they fortified themselves.

Sinan, after making an enquiry, disclaimed responsibility, and, persuading the Aleppines to withdraw, himself attacked and destroyed them. Other sources speak of similar groups of ecstatics in these years. It is probable that vague rumours and reports of these events underlie the later legend of the Assassins' Gardens of Paradise.

Once established, Sinan's first task was to consolidate his new realm. He rebuilt the fortresses of Rusafa and Khawabi, and rounded off his territory by capturing and refortifying Ulayqa. 'He built fortresses in Syria for the sect,' says an Arabic chronicler. 'Some were new and some were old ones which he had obtained by strategems and fortified and made inaccessible. Time spared him and kings took care not to attack his possessions for fear of the murderous attacks of his henchmen. He ruled in Syria for thirty odd years. Their Chief Missionary sent emissaries from Alamut a number of times to kill him, fearing his usurpation of the headship, and Sinan used to kill them. Some of them he deceived and dissuaded from carrying out their orders.'[11] This has been taken to mean that Sinan, alone among the Syrian Assassin leaders, threw off the authority of Alamut and pursued an entirely independent policy. For this view there is some support in the doctrinal fragments bearing his name, preserved into modern times among the Syrian Ismailis. These make no reference to Alamut, to its chiefs, or to the Nizari Imams, but acclaim Sinan himself as supreme and divine leader.

Our information about the policies of the Assassins under Sinan deals principally with a series of specific events in which they were involved: the two attempts on the life of Saladin, followed by his inconclusive attack on Masyaf; a murder and a fire in Aleppo; and the murder of Conrad of Montferrat. Apart from this there are only vague accounts of threatening letters to Nur al-Din and Saladin, and a reference by a Jewish traveller from Spain, Benjamin of Tudela, to a state of war in 1167 between the Assassins and the country of Tripoli.

The rise of Saladin as the architect of Muslim unity and orthodoxy and the champion of the holy war won him at first the position of chief enemy of the Assassins, and inevitably inclined them to look more favourably on the Zangids of Mosul and Aleppo, now his chief opponents. In letters written to the caliph in Baghdad in 1181-2, Saladin accuses the rulers of Mosul of being in league with the heretical Assassins and using their mediation with the unbelieving Franks. He speaks of their promising the Assassins castles, lands, and a house of propaganda in Aleppo, and of sending emissaries both to Sinan and to the Crusaders, and stresses his own role as defender of Islam against the threefold threat of Frankish unbelief, Assassin heresy, and Zangid treason. The author of the Ismaili biography of Sinan, himself affected by the holy war ideals of later times, depicts his hero as a collaborator of Saladin in the struggle against the Crusaders.

Both statements may be true for different dates. Though Saladin's account of the degree of collaboration among his opponents is probably exaggerated in order to discredit the Zangids, it was natural enough that his various enemies should at first concentrate their attacks on him rather than on one another. The curious story told by William of Tyre of an Assassin proposal to embrace Christianity may even reflect a genuine rapprochement between Sinan and the kingdom of Jerusalem.

The first Assassin attempt on Saladin's life occurred in December 1174 or January 1175, while he was besieging Aleppo. According to the biographers of Saladin, Gümüshtigin, who governed the city on behalf of the Zangid child who was its nominal ruler, sent messengers to Sinan, offering him lands and money in return for the assassination of Saladin. The appointed emissaries penetrated the camp on a cold winter day, but were recognized by the emir of Abu Qubais, a neighbour of theirs. He questioned them, and was at once killed. In the ensuing fracas many people were killed, but Saladin himself was unscathed. In the following year Sinan decided to make another attempt, and on 22 May 1176, Assassins, disguised as soldiers in his army, attacked him with knives while he was besieging Azaz. Thanks to his armour Saladin received only superficial wounds, and the assailants were dealt with by his emirs, several of whom perished in the struggle. Some sources attribute this second attempt also to the instigation of Gümüshtigin. After these events Saladin adopted elaborate precautions, sleeping in a specially constructed wooden tower and allowing no one whom he did not know personally to approach him.

While it is by no means impossible that, in organizing these two attempts on Saladin's life, Sinan was acting in concert with Gümüshtigin, it is unlikely that Gümüshtigin's inducements were his primary motive. What is far more probable is that Sinan, acting for reasons of his own, accepted the help of Gümüshtigin, thus gaining both material and tactical advantages. Similar considerations apply to the statement contained in a letter sent by Saladin to the caliph from Cairo in 1174, that the leaders of the abortive pro-Fatimid conspiracy in Egypt in that year had written to Sinan, stressing their common faith and urging him to take action against Saladin. The Nizari Ismailis of Syria and Persia owed no allegiance to the last Fatimids in Cairo, whom they regarded as usurpers. That Fatimid elements sought the aid of the Syrian Assassins is likely enough – some half-century previously the Fatimid caliph al-Amir had attempted to persuade them to accept his leadership. But the Nizaris had refused, and al-Amir himself had fallen to their daggers. It is not impossible that Sinan, again for tactical reasons, may have been willing to collaborate with the Egyptian conspirators, though it is unlikely that he would have continued to act in their interests after the definitive crushing of the plot in Egypt. A more likely immediate cause for Sinan's action against Saladin may be found in a story told by a later chronicler, though not by the extant contemporary authors. In 1174–5, according to this account, ten thousand horsemen of the Nubuwiyya, an anti-Shi'ite religious order in Iraq, raided the Ismaili centres in al-Bab and Buza'a, where they slaughtered 13,000 Ismailis and carried off much booty and many captives. Profiting from the confusion of the Ismailis, Saladin sent his army against them, raiding Sarmin, Ma'arrat Masrin, and Jabal al-Summaq, and killing most of the inhabitants. The chronicler unfortunately does not say in what month these events took place, but if, as seems likely, Saladin's raid was carried out while his army was on its way northward to Aleppo, it may serve to explain the hostility of the Assassins towards him. Even without this explanation, however, it is clear that the emergence of Saladin as the major power in Muslim Syria, with a policy of Muslim unification, would mark him down as a dangerous adversary.

In August 1176 Saladin advanced on the Assassin territories, in search of vengeance, and laid siege to Masyaf. There are different versions of the circumstances of his withdrawal. Saladin's secretary and historian Imad al-Din, followed by most of the other Arabic sources, attributes it to the mediation of Saladin's uncle, the prince of Hama, to whom his Assassin neighbours appealed for intercession. Another biographer adds a more convincing reason – the Frankish attack on the Biqa' valley, and the resulting urgent need for Saladin's presence there. In Kamal al-Din's history of Aleppo it is Saladin who invokes the mediation of the prince of Hama, and asks for peace, apparently as a result of the terror inspired by Assassin tactics. In the Ismaili version, Saladin is terrified by Sinan's supernatural powers; the prince of Hama intercedes on his behalf, and begs Sinan to allow him to depart in safety. Saladin agrees to withdraw, Sinan gives him a safe-conduct, and the two become the best of friends. The Ismaili account is obviously heavily overlaid with legend, but seems to contain this element of truth, that some sort of agreement was reached. Certainly we hear of no overt acts by the Assassins against Saladin after the withdrawal from Masyaf and there are even some hints of collusion.

The historians tell several stories, the purpose of which is to explain – perhaps to justify – Saladin's tolerance of the Assassins. On one occasion, it is said, the Sultan sent a threatening letter to the Assassin chief. His reply was as follows: 'We have read the gist and details of your letter, and taken note of its threats against us with words and deeds, and by God it is astonishing to find a a fly buzzing in an elephant's ear and a gnat biting statues. Others before you have said these things and we destroyed them and none could help them. Will you then annul the truth and give aid to the false? "Those who have done wrong will know to what end they will revert." [Qur'an, xxvi, 228]. If indeed your orders have gone forth to cut off my head and tear my castles from the solid mountains, these are false hopes and vain fantasies, for essentials are not destroyed by accidentals, as souls are not dissolved by diseases. But if we return to the exoteric, perceived by the senses, and leave aside the esoteric, perceived by the mind, we have a good example in the Prophet of God, who said: "No prophet suffered what I suffered." You know what happened to his line and family and party. But the situation has not changed and the cause has not failed and praise to God in the first and last. We are oppressed and not oppressors, deprived and not deprivers. When "the truth comes the false vanishes; verily the false is apt to vanish." [*Qur'an*, xvii, 23]. You know the outward aspect of our affairs and the quality of our men, what they can accomplish in an instant and how they seek the intimacy of death. "Say: — Wish then for death if you speak truth." [*Qur'an*, ii, 88]. The common proverb says: "Do you threaten a duck with the river?" Prepare means for disaster and don a garment against catastrophe; for I will defeat you from within your own ranks and take vengeance against you at your own place, and you will be as one who encompasses his own destruction, and "for God that is not of much account." [cf. *Qur'an*, xiv, 23]. When you read this letter of ours, be on the look out for us and be moderate of your state, and read the first of "the Bee" and the last of "Sad".'[12]

Even more startling is a story told by Kamal al-Din on the authority of his brother: 'My brother (God have mercy on him) told me that Sinan sent a messenger to Saladin (God have mercy on him) and ordered him to deliver his message only in private. Saladin had him searched, and when they found nothing dangerous on him he dismissed the assembly for him, leaving only a few people, and asked him to deliver his message. But he said: "My master ordered me not to deliver the message [unless in private]." Saladin then emptied the assembly of all save two Mamluks, and then said: "Give your message." He replied: "I have been ordered only to deliver it in private." Saladin said: "These two do not leave me. If you wish, deliver your message, and if not, return." He said: "Why do you not send away these two as you sent away the others?" Saladin replied: "I regard these as my own sons, and they and I are as one." Then the messenger turned to the two Mamluks and said: "If I ordered you in the name of my master to kill this Sultan, would you do so?" They answered yes, and drew their swords, saying: "Command us as you wish." Sultan Saladin (God have mercy on him) was astounded, and the messenger left, taking them with him. And thereupon Saladin (God have mercy on him) inclined to make peace with him and enter into friendly relations with him. And God knows best.'[13]

The next murder, on 31 August 1177, was of Shihab al-Din ibn al-Ajami, the vizier of the Zangid al-Malik al-Salih in Aleppo, and former vizier of Nur al-Din ibn Zangi. This assassination, which was accompanied by unsuccessful attempts on two of the vizier's henchmen, is attributed by the Syrian historians to the machinations of Gümüshtigin, who had forged the signature of al-Malik al-Salih on a letter to Sinan asking him to send murderers. The authority for this story is the confession of the Assassins, who claimed, when questioned, that they were only carrying out the orders of al-Malik al-Salih himself. The trick was allegedly discovered in the course of subsequent correspondence between al-Malik al-Salih and Sinan, and Gümüshtigin's enemies seized the opportunity to bring about his downfall. Whatever the truth of this story, the death of the vizier and the ensuing discord and mistrust cannot have been unwelcome to Saladin.

The quarrel between Aleppo and Sinan continued. In 1179–80 al-Malik al-Salih seized al-Hajira from the Assassins. Sinan's protests producing no result, he sent agents to Aleppo who set fire to the market places and wrought great damage. Not one of the incendiaries was apprehended – a fact which suggests that that they could still command local support in the city.

On 28 April 1192 they brought off their greatest coup – the murder of the Marquis Conrad of Montferrat, the King of Jerusalem, in Tyre. Most sources agree that the murderers disguised themselves as Christian monks and wormed their way into the confidence of the bishop and the marquis. Then, when an opportunity arose, they stabbed him to death. Saladin's envoy in Tyre reported that when the two Assassins were put to the question they confessed that the king of England had instigated the murder. In view of the testimony of most of the oriental and some of the occidental sources, there seems little doubt that some such confession was indeed made. Richard's obvious interest in the disappearance of the marquis, and the suspicious speed with which his protégé Count Henry of Champagne married the widow and succeeded to the throne of the Latin kingdom, lent some colour to the story – and one can readily understand that it found widespread credence at the time. But whether or not the Assassins were telling the truth when they confessed is another question. The Zangid historian Ibn al-Athir, for whose dislike of Saladin due allowance must be made, mentions the attribution to Richard simply as a belief current among the Franks. He himself names Saladin as the instigator, and even knows the sum of money paid to Sinan for the work. The plan was to kill both Richard himself and Conrad, but the murder of Richard proved impossible. The Ismaili biography attributes the initiative to Sinan, with the prior approval and co-operation of Saladin; but here too allowance must be made for the author's obvious desire to present his hero as a loyal collaborator of Saladin in the holy war. He adds the unlikely information that, in reward for this deed, Saladin granted the Assassins many privileges, including the right to set up houses of propaganda in Cairo, Damascus, Homs, Hama, Aleppo, and other cities. In this story we may perhaps discern an exaggerated recollection of some definite recognition accorded to the Assassins by Saladin in the period after the agreement at Masyaf. Imad al-Din, on the other hand, tells us that the murder was not opportune for Saladin, since Conrad, though himself one of the leaders of the Crusaders, was an enemy of the more redoubtable Richard, and was in communication with Saladin at the time of his death. Conrad's death freed Richard from anxiety and encouraged him to resume hostilities. Four months later he signed a truce with Saladin in which, at Saladin's request, the Assassin territories were included.

The murder of Conrad was Sinan's last achievement. In 1192–3 or 1193–4 the redoubtable Old Man of the Mountain himself died, and was succeeded by a Persian called Nasr. With the new chief the authority of Alamut seems to have been restored, and remained unshaken until after the Mongol conquest.

The names of several of the chief da'is at different dates are known to us from literary sources and from inscriptions in the Ismaili centres in Syria; most of them are specifically referred to as delegates of Alamut.

As subjects of Alamut, the Syrian Assassins were also affected by the new policies of Jalal al-Din Hasan III – the restoration of the law, and the alliance with the caliph in Baghdad. In 1211 the lord of Alamut sent messages to Syria, ordering his Syrian followers to build mosques and perform the ritual prayers, to avoid drink and drugs and other forbidden things, to observe the fast and all the prescriptions of the holy law.

Little is known of how the 'reform' influenced the religious beliefs and practices of the Assassins; the alliance with the Caliph does however seem to have affected their activities. It is striking that in Syria, in the presence of the enemies of Islam, no further assassinations of Muslims are recorded, though several Christians were still to fall. The first of these was Raymond, son of Bohemond IV of Antioch, who was killed in the church in Tortosa in 1213. His father, thirsting for vengeance, laid siege to the fortress of Khawabi. The Assassins, by now clearly on good terms with the successors of Saladin, appealed for help to the ruler of Aleppo, who sent an expedition to relieve them. His troops suffered a set-back at the hands of the Franks, but an appeal to his colleague in Damascus brought an army which compelled the enemy to raise the siege and withdraw.

In the meantime the Assassin chiefs had found a way of turning their reputation to good account. Under threat of assassination, they exacted payments from both Muslim and Christian rulers, even, it would seem, from temporary visitors to the Levant. In the year 1227, according to an Arabic source, the chief da'i Majd al-Din received envoys from the Emperor Frederick II, who had come to Palestine on a Crusade; they brought gifts worth almost 80,000 dinars. On the pretext that the road to Alamut was too dangerous because of the ravages of the Khorazmians, Majd al-Din kept the gifts in Syria and himself gave the Emperor the safe-conduct he required. At the same time, he took the precaution of sending an envoy to the ruler of Aleppo, to inform him of the Emperor's embassy and to ensure concerted action.

The Khorazmian danger may also explain another incident, said to have occurred earlier in the same year. According to this story, Majd al-Din sent an envoy to the Seljuq Sultan of Rum, in Konya, to demand that the regular annual tribute of 2,000 dinars, which the Sultan had previously sent to Alamut, should now be sent to him. The Sultan, in some uncertainty, sent a messenger to Alamut to consult Jalal al-Din; the lord of Alamut confirmed that he had assigned this money to Syria, and instructed the Sultan to pay it. He paid.

At about this time the Assassins themselves became tributary to the Knights Hospitallers. After the Emperor's mission, says the Arabic chronicler, the Hospitallers demanded tribute from the Assassins, who refused, saying: 'Your king the Emperor gives to us; will you then take from us?' The Hospitallers then attacked them and carried off much booty. The text does not make it clear whether the tribute to the Hospitallers dates from this event or was already in existence.[14]

An interesting indication of how far the Assassins had become a recognized and even an accepted part of the Syrian political scene is given by Ibn Wasil, himself a native of central Syria. In the year 1240 the qadi of Sinjar, Badr al-Din, incurred the wrath of the new Sultan. Fleeing through Syria, he sought and received asylum from the Assassins. Their chief at that time was a Persian called Taj al-Din, who had come from Alamut. Ibn Wasil does not hesitate to add that he knew him personally and was on terms of friendship with him. The same Taj al-Din is named in a Masyaf inscription dated Dhu'l Qa'da 646 (February or March 1249).

Only one group of events remains to be recorded before the political extinction of the Assassins in Syria – their dealings with St Louis. The story of an Assassin plot against St Louis while he was still a youth in France can, like all the other stories of Assassin activities in Europe, be dismissed as without foundation. But the account by Joinville, the biographer of St Louis, of the king's dealings with the Assassins after his arrival in Palestine is of a different order, and bears every mark of authenticity. Emissaries of the Assassins came to the king in Acre, and asked him to pay tribute to their chief, 'as the Emperor of Germany, the King of Hungary, the Sultan of Babylon [Egypt], and the others do every year, because they know well they can only live as long as it may please him.'[15] Alternatively, if the King did not wish to pay tribute, they would be satisfied with the remission of the tribute which they themselves paid to the Hospitallers and the Templars. This tribute was paid, explains Joinville, because these two orders feared nothing from the Assassins, since, if one master was killed, he would at once be replaced by another as good and the Assassin chief did not wish to waste his men where nothing could be gained. In the event, the tribute to the orders continued, and the King and the chief da'i exchanged gifts. It was on this occasion that the Arabic-speaking friar Yves the Breton met and talked with the Assassin chief.

The end of the power of the Assassins came under the double assault of the Mongols and of the Mamluk Sultan of Egypt, Baybars. In Syria, as one would expect, the Assassins joined with the other Muslims in repelling the Mongol threat, and sought to win the good graces of Baybars by sending him embassies and gifts. Baybars at first showed no open hostility to them, and, in granting a truce to the Hospitallers in 1266, stipulated that they renounce the tribute they were receiving from various Muslim cities and districts, including the Assassin castles, whose tribute is given by an Egyptian source as 1,200 dinars and a hundred *mudd* of wheat and barley. The Assassins prudently sent emissaries to Baybars offering him the tribute which they had formerly paid to the Franks, to be used in the holy war.

But Baybars, whose life-work was the liberation of the Muslim Near East from the double threat of the Christian Franks and the heathen Mongols, could not be expected to tolerate the continued independence of a dangerous pocket of heretics and murderers in the very heart of Syria. As early as 1260 his biographer reports him as assigning the Assassin lands in fief to one of his generals. In 1265 he ordered the collection of taxes and tolls from the 'gifts' brought for the Assassins from the various princes who paid them tribute. Among them the sources name 'the Emperor, Alfonso, the Kings of the Franks and the Yemen'.[16] The Assassins, weakened in Syria and disheartened by the fate of their Persian brothers, were in no position to resist. Meekly accepting this measure, they themselves paid tribute to Baybars, and soon it was he, in place of the fallen lord of Alamut, who appointed and dismissed them at will.

In 1270 Baybars, dissatisfied with the attitude of the aged chief Najm al-Din, deposed him and appointed in his place his more compliant son-in-law Sarim al-Din Mubarak, Assassin governor of Ulayqa. The new chief, who held his office as representative of Baybars, was excluded from Masyaf, which came under the direct rule of Baybars. But Sarim al-Din, by a trick, won possession of Masyaf. Baybars dislodged him and sent him as a prisoner to Cairo where he died, probably poisoned, and the now chastened Najm al-Din was re-appointed, conjointly with his son Shams al-Din, in return for an annual tribute. They are both named in an inscription in the mosque of Qadmus, of about this date.

In February or March 1271 Baybars arrested two Assassins who, allegedly, had been sent to murder him. They had gone, it was said, on an embassy from Ulayqa to Bohemond VI of Tripoli, and he had arranged for them to assassinate the Sultan. Shams al-Din was arrested and charged with intelligence with the Franks, but released after his father Najm al-Din had come to plead his innocence. The two would-be murderers were set free; the two Ismaili leaders, under pressure, agreed to surrender their castles and live at Baybars' court. Najm al-Din accompanied Baybars, and died in Cairo early in 1274. Shams al-Din was allowed to go to Kahf 'to settle its affairs'. Once there, he began to organize resistance, but in vain. In May and June 1271 Baybars' lieutenants seized Ulayqa and Rusafa and in October Shams al-Din, realizing his cause was hopeless, surrendered to Baybars. At first he was well received. Later, learning of a plot to assassinate some of his emirs, Baybars deported Shams al-Din and his party to Egypt. The blockade of the castles continued.

Khawabi fell in the same year, and the remaining castles were all occupied by 1273.

With the submission of the Assassins to Baybars, their skilled services seem to have been, for a short time, at his disposal. As early as April 1271 Baybars is reported as threatening the Count of Tripoli with assassination. The attempt on Prince Edward of England in 1272 and perhaps also the murder of Philip of Montfort in Tyre in 1270 were instigated by him. Some later chroniclers also speak of the employment of Assassins, by Mamluk Sultans, to remove troublesome opponents, and the fourteenth century Moorish traveller Ibn Battuta even gives a description of the arrangements. 'When the Sultan wishes to send one of them to kill an enemy, he pays them the price of his blood. If the murderer escapes after performing his task, the money is his; if he is caught, his children get it. They use poisoned knives to strike down their appointed victims. Sometimes their plots fail, and they themselves are killed.'[17]

Such stories are probably the offspring of legend and suspicion, of no more significance than the tales that were being told further west, of murders arranged for the princes of Europe, at a price. by the Old Man of the Mountain. After the thirteenth century, there are no further authenticated murders by Syrian Assassins acting for the sect. Henceforth Ismailism stagnated as a minor heresy in Persia and Syria, with little or no political importance. In the fourteenth century a split occurred in the line of Nizari Imams. The Syrian and Persian Ismailis followed different claimants, and from that date onwards ceased to maintain contact with one another.

In the sixteenth century, after the Ottoman conquest of Syria, the first surveys of land and population prepared for the new masters duly record the qilā' al-da'wa – castles of the mission – a group of villages west of Hama, including such old and famous centres as Qadmus and Kahf, and inhabited by followers of a peculiar sect. They are distinguished only by the fact that they pay a special tax.[18] They do not reappear on the pages of history until the early nineteenth century, when they are reported in normal conflict with their rulers, their neighbours and one another. From the mid-century they settled down as a peaceful rural population, with their centre at Salamiyya, a new settlement reclaimed by them from the desert. At the present time they number some 50,000, of whom some, but not all, have accepted the Aga Khan as their Imam.

6

Means and Ends

The Ismaili Assassins did not invent assassination; they merely lent it their name. Murder as such is as old as the human race; its antiquity is strikingly symbolized in the fourth chapter of Genesis, where the first murderer and the first victim appear as brothers, the children of the first man and woman. Political murder comes with the emergence of political authority – when power is vested in an individual, and the removal of that individual is seen as a quick and simple method of effecting political change. Usually the motive for such murders is personal, factional or dynastic – the replacement of an individual, a party or a family by another in the possession of power. Such murders are commonplace in autocratic kingdoms and empires, in both East and West.

Sometimes the murder is conceived – by others as well as the murderer – as a duty, and is justified by ideological arguments. The victim is a tyrant or a usurper; to kill him is a virtue, not a crime. Such ideological justification may be expressed in political or religious terms – in many societies there is little difference between the two. In ancient Athens two friends, Harmodius and Aristogeiton, conspired to kill the tyrant Hippias. They succeeded only in killing his brother and co-ruler, and were both put to death. After the fall of Hippias, they became public heroes in Athens, celebrated in statuary and song; their descendants enjoyed privileges and exemptions. This idealization of tyrannicide became part of the political ethos of Greece and Rome, and found expression in such famous murders as those of Philip II of Macedon, Tiberius Gracchus and Julius Caesar. The same ideal appears among the Jews, in such figures as Ehud and Jehu, and, most dramatically, in the story of the beautiful Judith, who made her way to the tent of the oppressor Holofernes, and cut off his head as he slept. The book of Judith was written during the period of Hellenistic domination, and survives only in a Greek version; the Jews, followed by the Protestants, reject it as apocryphal. It is, however, included in the canon of the Roman Catholic Church, and has inspired many Christian painters and sculptors. Though Judith has no place in Jewish religious tradition, the ideal of pious murder which she represents survived to inspire the famous Sicarii, or dagger-men – a group of zealots who appeared about the time of the fall of Jerusalem, and devoutly destroyed those who opposed or hindered them.

Regicide – both practical and idealistic – was familiar from the very beginnings of Islamic political history. Of the four Righteous Caliphs who followed the Prophet in the headship of the Islamic community, three were murdered. The second Caliph, Umar, was stabbed by a Christian slave with a private grievance; learning this, the Caliph on his deathbed thanked God that he had not been murdered by one of the faithful. Even this consolation was denied to his successors Uthman and Ali, who were both struck down by Muslim Arabs – the first by a group of angry mutineers, the second by a religious fanatic. In both murders, the perpetrators saw themselves as tyrannicides, freeing the community from an unrighteous ruler – and both found others to agree with them.

The issues crystallized in the course of the Muslim civil war that followed Uthman's death. Mu'awiya, the governor of Syria and kinsman of the murdered Caliph, demanded the punishment of the regicides. Ali, who had succeeded as Caliph, was unable or unwilling to comply, and his supporters, to justify his inaction, claimed that no crime had been committed. Uthman had been an oppressor; his death was an execution, not a murder.[1] The same argument was used by the extremist sect of the Kharijites to justify the murder of Ali himself a few years later.

To some extent, Islamic tradition gives recognition to the principle of justifiable revolt. While conceding autocratic powers to the sovereign, it lays down that the subject's duty of obedience lapses where the command is sinful, and that 'there must be no obedience to a creature against his Creator'. Since no procedure is laid down for testing the righteousness of a command, or for exercising the right to disobey one that is sinful, the only effective recourse for the conscientious subject is to rebel against the ruler, and try to overrule or depose him by force. A more expeditious procedure is to remove him by assassination. This principle was often invoked, especially by sectarian rebels, to justify their acts.

In fact, after the death of Ali and accession of Mu'awiya, the murder of rulers becomes rare, and when it occurs is usually dynastic rather than revolutionary in inspiration. On the contrary, the Shi'a claimed that it was their Imams, and other members of the house of the Prophet, who were being murdered at the instigation of the Sunni Caliphs; their literature includes long lists of Alid martyrs, whose blood called for vengeance.

In sending their emissaries to kill the unrighteous and their minions, the Ismailis could thus invoke an old Islamic tradition. It was a tradition which was never dominant, and had for long been dormant, but which had its place, especially within the circle of the dissident and extremist sects.

The ancient ideal of tyrannicide, the religious obligation to rid the world of an unrighteous ruler, certainly contributed to the practice of assassination, as adopted and applied by the Ismailis. But there was more to it than that. The killing by the Assassin of his victim was not only an act of piety; it also had a ritual, almost a sacramental quality. It is significant that in all their murders, in both Persia and Syria, the Assassins always used a dagger; never poison,[2] never missiles, though there must have been occasions when these would have been easier and safer. The Assassin is almost always caught, and usually indeed makes no attempt to escape; there is even a suggestion that to survive a mission was shameful. The words of a twelfth-century Western author are revealing: 'When therefore any of them have chosen to die in this way . . . he himself [i.e. the Chief] hands them knives which are, so to speak, consecrated . . .'[3]

Human sacrifice and ritual murder have no place in Islamic law, tradition or practice. Yet both are ancient and deep-rooted in human societies, and can reappear in unexpected places. Just as the forgotten dance-cults of antiquity, in defiance of the austere worship of Islam, reappear in the ecstatic ritual of the dancing dervishes, so do the ancient cults of death find new expressions in Islamic terms. In the early eighth century, the Muslim authors tell us, a man called Abu Mansur al-Ijli, of Kufa, claimed to be the Imam, and taught that the prescriptions of the law had a symbolic meaning, and need not be obeyed in their literal sense. Heaven and Hell had no separate existence, but were merely the pleasures and misfortunes of this world. His followers practised murder as a religious duty. Similar doctrines – and practices – were ascribed to his contemporary and fellow-tribesman Mughira b. Sa'id. Both groups were suppressed by the authorities. It is significant that they were restricted, according to their beliefs, to a single weapon in their murderous rites. One group strangled their victims with nooses; another clubbed them with wooden cudgels. Only with the coming of the Mahdi would they be permitted to use steel.[4] Both groups belonged to the extreme fringe of the extremist Shi'a. The parallel they offer to both the antinomianism and the weapon-cult of the later Ismailis is striking.

As custodians of esoteric mysteries for the initiate, as purveyors of salvation through knowledge of the Imam, as bearers of a promise of messianic fulfilment, of release from the toils of the world and the yoke of the law, the Ismailis are part of a long tradition, that goes back to the beginnings of Islam and far beyond, and forward to our own day – a tradition of popular and emotional cults in sharp contrast with the learned and legal religion of the established order.

There were many such sects and groups before the Ismailis, but theirs was the first to create an effective and enduring organization. It was a sign of the times. The earlier sodalities of the poor and powerless were scattered and insignificant, and rarely achieved the literary mention which alone could make them known to the historian. In the atomized and insecure society of the later Caliphate, men sought comfort and assurance in new and stronger forms of association; these became more numerous and more extensive, and reached from the lower to the middle and even the upper levels of the population – until finally the Caliph al-Nasir himself, by ceremonially joining one of them, tried to incorporate them in the apparatus of government.

These associations were of many kinds. Some were primarily regional, based on cities or quarters, with civic, police or even military functions. Some, in a society where crafts often coincided with local, ethnic, or religious groups, may also have acquired an economic role. Often they appear as associations of youths or young men, with ranks and rites to mark the attainment of adolescence and of manhood. Most were religious brotherhoods, the followers of holy men and of the cults established by them. Common features were the adoption of beliefs and practices belonging to popular religion and mistrusted by orthodoxy; a close bond of loyalty to comrades and devotion to leaders; a system of initiation and of hierarchic grades, supported by elaborate symbols and ceremonials. Most of these groups, though vaguely dissident, were politically inactive. The Ismailis, with their militant tactics and revolutionary aims, were able to use this form of organization for a sustained attempt to overthrow and replace the existing order. At the same time, they gradually abandoned the philosophical refinements of their earlier doctrines, and adopted forms of religion that were closer to the beliefs current among the brotherhoods. In one respect, according to the Persian historians, the Ismailis adopted an almost monastic rule; the commandants of their castles, as long as they held office, had no women with them.

In one respect the Assassins are without precedent – in the planned, systematic and long-term use of terror as a political weapon. The stranglers of Iraq had been small-scale and random practitioners, rather like the thugs of India, with whom they may be connected. Previous political murders, however dramatic, were the work of individuals or at best of small groups of plotters limited in both purpose and effect. In the skills of murder and conspiracy, the Assassins have countless predecessors; even in the refinement of murder as an art, a rite, and a duty, they have been anticipated or prefigured. But they may well be the first terrorists. 'Brothers', says an Ismaili poet, 'when the time of triumph comes, with good fortune from both worlds as our companion, then by one single warrior on foot a king may be stricken with terror, though he own more than a hundred thousand horsemen.'[5]

It was true. For centuries the Shi'a had squandered their zeal and blood for their Imams, without avail. There had been countless risings, ranging from the self-immolation of small groups of ecstatics to carefully planned military operations. All but a few had failed, crushed by the armed forces of a state and an order that they were too weak to overthrow. Even the very few that succeeded brought no release for the pent-up emotion that they expressed. Instead, the victors, once invested with the panoply of authority and the custodianship of the Islamic community, turned against their own supporters and destroyed them.

Hasan-i Sabbah knew that his preaching could not prevail against the entrenched orthodoxy of Sunni Islam — that his followers could not meet and defeat the armed might of the Seljuq state. Others before him had vented their frustration in unplanned violence, in hopeless insurrection, or in sullen passivity. Hasan found a new way, by which a small force, disciplined and devoted, could strike effectively against an overwhelmingly superior enemy. 'Terrorism', says a modern authority, 'is carried on by a narrowly limited organization and is inspired by a sustained program of large-scale objectives in the name of which terror is practised.'[6] This was the method that Hasan chose – the method, it may well be, that he invented.

'The Old Man of the Mountain,' says Joinville, speaking of a later Ismaili chief in Syria, 'paid tribute to the Templars and the Hospitallers, because they feared nothing from the Assassins, since the Old Man could gain nothing if he caused the Master of the Temple or of the Hospital to be killed; for he knew very well that if he had one killed, another just as good would replace him, and for this reason he did not wish to lose Assassins where he could gain nothing (see above, p. 121).'[7] The two orders of knighthood were integrated institutions, with an institutional structure, hierarchy and loyalty, which made them immune to attack by assassination; it was the absence of these qualities that made the atomized Islamic state, with centralized, autocratic power based on personal and transient loyalties, peculiarly vulnerable to it.

Hasan-i Sabbah showed political genius in perceiving this weakness of the Islamic monarchies. He also displayed remarkable administrative and strategic gifts in exploiting it by terrorist attack.

For such a campaign of sustained terror there were two obvious requirements – organization and ideology. There had to be an organization capable both of launching the attack and surviving the inevitable counter-blow; there had to be a system of belief – which in that time and place could only be a religion – to inspire and sustain the attackers to the point of death.

Both were found. The reformed Ismaili religion, with its memories of passion and martyrdom, its promise of divine and human fulfilment, was a cause that gave dignity and courage to those that embraced it, and inspired a devotion unsurpassed in human history. It was the loyalty of the Assassins, who risked and even courted death for their Master, that first attracted the attention of Europe, and made their name a by-word for faith and self-sacrifice before it became a synonym for murderer.

There was cool planning, as well as fanatical zeal, in the work of the Assassins. Several principles are discernible. The seizure of castles – some of them the former lairs of robber-chieftains – provided them with safe bases; the rule of secrecy – adapted from the old doctrine of *taqiyya* – helped both security and solidarity. The work of the terrorists was supported by both religious and political action. Ismaili missionaries found or gained sympathizers among the rural and urban population; Ismaili envoys called on highly-placed Muslims, whose fears or ambitions might make them temporary allies of the cause.

Such alliances raise an important general issue concerning the Assassins. Of several score murders recorded in Iran and Syria, a fair number are said by one or another source to have been instigated by third parties, often with an offer of money or other inducements. Sometimes the story is based on an alleged confession by the actual murderers, when caught and put to the question.

Clearly the Assassins, the devoted servants of a religious cause, were not mere cut-throats with daggers for hire. They had their own political objective, the establishment of the true Imamate, and neither they nor their leaders are likely to have been the tools of other men's ambitions. Yet the persistent and widespread stories of complicity, involving such names as Berkyaruq and Sanjar in the East, Saladin and Richard Coeur de Lion in the West, require some explanation.

Some of these stories were current because they were true. In many periods and places, there have been ambitious men who were willing to enlist the aid of violent extremists; they may not have shared or even liked their beliefs, but they thought they could use them, in the hope, usually misplaced, that they would be able to abandon these dangerous allies when they had served their purpose. Such was Ridwan of Aleppo, a Seljuq prince who did not scruple to switch from a Sunni to a Fatimid allegiance, and then to welcome the Assassins to his city, as a support against his kinsmen and his overlord. Such too were the scheming viziers in Isfahan and Damascus, who tried to use the power and terror of the Assassins for their own advancement. Sometimes the motive was terror rather than ambition – as for example with the pathetically frightened vizier of the Khorazmshah Jalal al-Din, described by Nasawi (see above, p. 85). Soldiers and sultans, as well as viziers, could be terrified into compliance, and several of the most dramatic stories that are told of Assassin skill and daring seem to have as their purpose to justify some tacit understanding between a pious Sunni monarch and the Ismaili revolutionaries.

The motives of men like Sanjar and Saladin are somewhat more complex. Both made their accommodations with the Assassins; neither is likely to have been swayed purely by personal fear or personal ambition. Both were engaged on great tasks – Sanjar on the restoration of the Seljuq Sultanate and the defence of Islam against heathen invaders from the East, Saladin on the renewal of Sunni unity and the ejection of Christian invaders from the West. Both must have realized the truth – that after their own deaths their kingdoms would crumble and their plans come to nothing. They may well have felt that a temporary concession to what was ultimately a less dangerous enemy was justified, in order to secure their personal safety, and with it the chance to complete their great work for the restoration and defence of Islam.

For the Assassins themselves, the calculation was much simpler. Their purpose was to disrupt and destroy the Sunni order; if some Sunni leaders could be tempted or terrorized into helping them, so much the better. Even in the days of their early fury, the Assassin leaders never disdained the help of others when it was forthcoming; later, when they became in effect territorial rulers, they fitted their policies with skill and ease into the complex mosaic of alliances and rivalries of the Muslim world.

All this does not mean that their services were for sale, or that every story of complicity, even those supported by confessions, was true. The leaders might make secret arrangements, but it is unlikely that they would inform the actual murderer of the details. What is much more probable is that the Assassin setting out on a mission was given what in modern parlance would be called a 'cover story', implicating the likeliest character on the scene. This would have the additional advantage of sowing mistrust and suspicion in the opposing camp. The murders of the Caliph al-Mustarshid and the Crusader Conrad of Montferrat are good examples of this. The suspicion thrown on Sanjar in Persia and on Richard among the Crusaders must have served a useful purpose in confusing the issues and creating discord. In addition, we cannot be sure that every murder ascribed to or even claimed by the Assassins was in fact committed by them. Murder, for private or public reasons, was at least normally common, and the Assassins themselves must have provided 'cover' for a number of unideological assassinations in which they had no part.

The Assassins chose their victims with care. Some Sunni authors have suggested that they waged indiscriminate war against the whole Muslim community. 'It is well-known and established,' says Hamdullah Mustawfi, 'that the Batinis [i.e. the Ismailis], may they get their just deserts, neglect no moment in injuring the Muslims in whatever way they can, and believe that they will receive rich reward and bounteous recompense for this. To commit no murder and to subdue no victim they regard as a great sin.'8 Hamdullah, writing in about 1330, presents a later view, contaminated by the myths and legends that were already current. The contemporary sources in both Persia and Syria suggest that the Ismaili terror was directed against specific persons, for specific purposes, and that apart from a few, quite exceptional outbreaks of mob violence, their relations with their Sunni neighbours were fairly normal. This seems to be true both of the Ismaili minorities in the towns, and of the Ismaili territorial rulers, in their dealings with their Sunni colleagues.

The victims of the Assassins belong to two main groups; the first of princes, officers and ministers, the second of qadis and other religious dignitaries. An intermediate group between the two, the city prefects, also received occasional attention. With few exceptions, the victims were Sunni Muslims. The Assassins did not normally attack Twelver or other Shi'ites, nor did they turn their daggers against native Christians or Jews. There are few attacks even on the Crusaders in Syria, and most of them seem to follow Sinan's accord with Saladin and Hasan's alliance with the Caliph.

The enemy, for the Ismailis, was the Sunni establishment – political and military, bureaucratic and religious. Their murders were designed to frighten, to weaken, and ultimately to overthrow it. Some were simply acts of vengeance and warning, such as the killing, in their own mosques, of Sunni divines who had spoken or acted against them. Other victims were chosen for more immediate and more specific reasons – such as the commanders of armies attacking the Ismailis, or the occupants of strongholds that they wished to acquire. Tactical and propagandist motives combine in the murder of major figures, such as the great vizier Nizam al-Mulk, two Caliphs, and the attempts on Saladin.

It is much more difficult to determine the nature of Ismaili support. Much of it must have come from the countryside. The Ismailis had their main bases in castles; they were most successful when they could rely on the population of the surrounding villages for support and also for recruitment. In both Persia and Syria the Ismaili emissaries tried to establish themselves in areas where there were old traditions of religious deviation. Such traditions are remarkably persistent, and have survived, in some of these areas, to the present day. Some of the religious writings of the New Preaching, in contrast with the sophisticated urban intellectualism of Fatimid theology, show many of the magical qualities associated with peasant religion.

Ismaili support could be most effectively mobilized and directed in rural and mountain areas. It was not, however, limited to such areas. Clearly, the Ismailis also had their followers in the towns, where they gave discreet help when needed to the men from the castles proceeding on their missions. Sometimes, as in Isfahan and Damascus, they were strong enough to come out into the open in the struggle for power.

It has usually been assumed that the urban supporters of Ismailism were drawn from the lower orders of society – the artisans, and below them the floating, restless rabble. This assumption is based on the occasional references to Ismaili activists of such social origin, and to the general lack of evidence on Ismaili sympathies among the better-off classes, even those that were at some disadvantage in the Seljuq Sunni order. There are many signs of shi'ite sympathies among the merchants and literati, for example – but they seem to have preferred the passive dissent of the Twelvers to the radical subversion of the Ismailis.

Inevitably, many of the leaders and teachers of the Ismailis were educated townsmen. Hasan-i Sabbah was from Rayy, and received a scribal education; Ibn Attash was a physician, as was the first emissary of Alamut in Syria. Sinan was a schoolmaster, and, according to his own statement, the son of a family of notables in Basra. Yet the New Preaching never seems to have had the seductive intellectual appeal that had tempted poets, philosophers and theologians in earlier times. From the ninth to the eleventh centuries Ismailism, in its various forms, had been a major intellectual force in Islam, a serious contender for the minds as well as the hearts of the believers, and had even gained the sympathy of such a towering intellect as the philosopher and scientist Avicenna (980–1037). In the twelfth and thirteenth centuries this is palpably no longer true. After Nasir-i Khusraw, who died some time after 1087, there is no major intellectual figure in Ismaili theology, and even his followers were limited to peasants and mountaineers in remote places. Under Hasan-i Sabbah and his successors, the Ismailis pose terrible political, military and social problems to Sunni Islam, but they no longer offer an intellectual challenge. More and more, their religion acquires the magical and emotional qualities, the redemptionist and millenarian hopes, associated with the cults of the dispossessed, the disprivileged and the unstable. Ismaili theology had ceased to be, and did not again become, a serious alternative to the new orthodoxy that was dominating the intellectual life of the Muslim cities – though Ismaili spiritual concepts and attitudes continued, in a disguised and indirect form, to influence Persian and Turkish mysticism and poetry, and elements of Ismailism may be discerned in such later outbreaks of revolutionary messianism as the dervish revolt in fifteenth-century Turkey and the Babi upheaval in ninteenth-century Persia.

There is one more question that the modern historian is impelled to ask – what does it mean? In religious terms, the New Preaching of the Ismailis can be seen as a resurgence of certain millenarian and antinomian trends, which are recurrent in Islam and which have parallels – and perhaps antecedents – in other religious traditions. But when modern man ceased to accord first place to religion in his own concerns, he also ceased to believe that other men, in other times, could ever truly have done so, and so he began to re-examine the great religious movements of the past in search of interests and motives acceptable to modern minds.

The first great theory on the 'real' significance of Muslim heresy was launched by the Count de Gobineau, the father of modern racialism. For him, Shi'ism represented a reaction of the Indo-European Persians against Arab domination – against the constricting Semitism of Arab Islam. To nineteenth-century Europe, obsessed with the problems of national conflict and national freedom, such an explanation seemed reasonable and indeed obvious. The Shi'a stood for Persia, fighting first against

Arab and later against Turkish domination. The Assassins represented a form of militant, nationalist extremism, like the terrorist secret societies of nineteenth-century Italy and Macedonia.

The advance of scholarship on the one hand, and changes in European circumstances on the other, led in the twentieth century to some modifications in this theory of racial or national conflict. Increased knowledge showed that Shi'ism in general, and Ismailism in particular, were by no means exclusively Persian. The sect had begun in Iraq; the Fatimid caliphate had achieved its major successes in Arabia, in North Africa and in Egypt – and even the reformed Ismailism of Hasan-i Sabbah, though launched in Persia and by Persians, had won an extensive following in Arab Syria and had even percolated among the Turcoman tribes that had migrated into the Middle East from Central Asia. And in any case, nationality was no longer regarded as a sufficient base for great historical movements.

In a series of studies the first of which appeared in 1911, a Russian scholar, V. V. Barthold, offered another explanation. In his view, the real meaning of the Assassin movement was a war of the castles against the cities – a last, and ultimately unsuccessful attempt by the rural Iranian aristocracy to resist the new, urban social order of Islam. Pre-Islamic Persia had been a knightly society, to which the city had come as an Islamic innovation. Like the barons – and robber-barons – of mediaeval Europe, the Persian land-owning knights, with the support of the village population, waged war from their castles against this alien and encroaching new order. The Assassins were a weapon in this war.

Later Russian scholars revised and refined Barthold's attempt at an economic explanation of Ismailism. The Ismailis were not against the towns as such, in which they had their own supporters, but against certain dominant elements in the towns – the rulers and the military and civil notables, the new feudal lords and the officially favoured divines. Moreover the Ismailis could not simply be equated with the old nobility. They did not inherit their castles, but seized them, and their support came not so much from those who still owned their estates, as from those who had lost them to new owners – to the tax-farmers, officials and officers who had received grants of land and revenues from the new rulers at the expense of the gentry and peasantry. One view sees Ismailism as a reactionary ideology, devised by the great feudal magnates to defend their privileges against the equalitarianism of Sunni Islam; another as a response, varied according to circumstances, to the needs of the different groups which had suffered from the imposition of the Seljuq new order, and thus embracing both the deposed old ruling class and the discontented populace of the cities; yet another simply as a 'popular' movement based on the artisans, the city poor, and the peasantry of mountain regions. According to this view, Hasan's proclamation of the Resurrection was a victory of the 'popular' forces; his threats of punishment against those who still observed the Holy Law were directed against feudal elements in the Ismaili possessions, who were secretly faithful to Islamic orthodoxy and hostile to social equality.[9]

Like the earlier attempts at an ethnic explanation, these theories of economic determination have enriched our knowledge of Ismailism, by directing research into new and profitable directions; like earlier theologies, they have suffered from excessive dogmatism, which has stressed some aspects and neglected others – in particular the sociology of religion, of leadership, and of association. It is obvious that some extension of our knowledge of Islam and its sects, some refinement of our methods of enquiry, are needed before we can decide how significant was the economic element in Ismailism, and what precisely it was. In the meantime both the experience of events and the advance of scholarship in our own time may suggest that it is not so easy to disentangle national from economic factors, or either from psychic and social determinants, and that the distinction, so important to our immediate predecessors, between the radical right and the radical left may sometimes prove illusory.

No single, simple explanation can suffice to clarify the complex phenomenon of Ismailism, in the complex society of mediaeval Islam. The Ismaili religion evolved over a long period and a wide area, and meant different things at different times and places;

the Ismaili states were territorial principalities, with their own internal differences and conflicts; the social and economic order of the Islamic Empire, as of other mediaeval societies, was an intricate and changing pattern of different elites, estates, and classes, of social, ethnic and religious groups – and neither the religion nor the society in which it appeared has yet been adequately explored.

Like other great historic creeds and movements, Ismailism drew on many sources, and served many needs. For some, it was a means of striking at a hated domination, whether to restore an old order or to create a new one; for others, the only way of achieving God's purpose on earth. For different rulers, it was a device to secure and maintain local independence against alien interference, or a road to the Empire of the world; a passion and a fulfilment, that brought dignity and meaning to drab and bitter lives, or a gospel of release and destruction; a return to ancestral truths – and a promise of future illumination.

Concerning the place of the Assassins in the history of Islam, four things may be said with reasonable assurance. The first is that their movement, whatever its driving force may have been, was regarded as a profound threat to the existing order, political, social and religious; the second is that they are no isolated phenomenon, but one of a long series of messianic movements, at once popular and obscure, impelled by deep-rooted anxieties, and from time to time exploding in outbreaks of revolutionary violence; the third is that Hasan-i Sabbah and his followers succeeded in reshaping and redirecting the vague desires, wild beliefs and aimless rage of the discontented into an ideology and an organization which, in cohesion, discipline and purposive violence, have no parallel in earlier or in later times. The fourth, and perhaps ultimately the most significant point, is their final and total failure. They did not overthrow the existing order; they did not even succeed in holding a single city of any size. Even their castle domains became no more than petty principalities, which in time were overwhelmed by conquest, and their followers have become small and peaceful communities of peasants and merchants – one sectarian minority among many.

Yet the undercurrent of messianic hope and revolutionary violence which had impelled them flowed on, and their ideals and methods found many imitators. For these, the great changes of our time have provided new causes for anger, new dreams of fulfilment, and new tools of attack.

Notes

Abbreviations

BIE   Bulletin de l'Institut égyptien (d'Egypte)
BIFAO   Bulletin de l'Institut français d'archéologie orientale
BSOAS   Bulletin of the School of Oriental [and African] Studies
EI(1)   Encyclopaedia of Islam, 1st edition
EI(2)   Encyclopaedia of Islam, 2nd edition
IC   Islamic Culture
JA   Journal asiatique
JAOS   Journal of the American Oriental Society
JBBRAS   Journal of the Bombay Branch of the Royal Asiatic
           Society
RCASJ   Royal Central Asian Society Journal
REI   Revue des études islamiques
RHC   Recueil des historiens des Croisades
s.   Persian Solar year
SI   Studia Islamica
ZDMG   Zeitschrift der Deutschen Morgenländischen Gesellschaft

Transcription

Diacritical marks have been omitted from the text, but are retained, for the convenience of the specialist reader, in the notes and index. The transcription in the passages cited from published translations has been slightly modified to accord with the system used in this book.

Chapter 1   (pages 1–19)

The treatment of the Assassins in mediaeval Western literature has been discussed by C. E. Nowell, 'The Old Man of the Mountain', in *Speculum*, xxii (1947), 497–519, and by L. Olschki, *Storia letteraria delle scoperte geografiche*, Florence 1937, 215–22. A brief survey of Western scholarship on the Assassins and related sects is included in B. Lewis, 'The sources for the history of the Syrian Assassins', in *Speculum*, xxvii (1952), 475–89. Bibliographies of Ismaili studies were prepared by Asaf A. A. Fyzee, 'Materials for an Ismaili bibliography: 1920–34', in *JBBRAS*, NS. xi (1935), 59–65, 'Additional notes for an Ismaili bibliography', *ibid.*, xii (1936), 107–9; and 'Materials for an Ismaili bibliography: 1936–1938', *ibid.*, xvi (1940), 99–101. More recent articles (but not books) are listed in J. D. Pearson, *Index Islamicus 1906–1955*, Cambridge 1958, 89–90, and *Supplement*, Cambridge 1962, 29. On the origins and use of the term reference may be made to the standard etymological and historical dictionaries of English, French, Italian and other European languages, and to the article 'Ḥashīshiyya' in *EI*(2).

1   Brocardus, *Directorium ad passagium faciendum*, in *RHC*, E, *Documents arméniens*, ii, Paris 1906, 496–7.

2   Villani, *Cronica*, ix, 290–1; Dante, *Inferno*, xix, 49–50; cit. in *Vocabulario della lingua italiana*, s.v. assassino.

3   The report of Gerhard (possibly, as the editor suggests, an error for Burchard), *vice-dominus* of Strasburg, is cited by the German chronicler Arnold of Lübeck in his *Chronicon Slavorum*, vii, 8 (ed. W. Wattenbach, *Deutschlands Geschichtsquellen*, Stuttgart–Berlin 1907, ii, 240).

4   William of Tyre, *Historia rerum in partibus transmarinis gestarum*, xx, 31, ed. J. P. Migne, *Patrologia*, cci, Paris 1903, 810–1; cf. English translation by E. A. Babcock and A. C. Krey, *A history of deeds done beyond the sea*, ii, New York 1943, 391.

5   *Chronicon*, iv, 16, ed. Wattenbach, 178–9.

6   F. M. Chambers, 'The troubadours and the Assassins', in *Modern Language Notes*, lxiv (1949), 245–51. Olschki notes a similar passage in a sonnet probably written by Dante in his youth, in which the poet describes the devotion of the lover to his love as greater than that of the Assassin to the Old Man or the priest to God (*Storia*, 215).

7   Cont. William of Tyre, xxiv, 27, ed. Migne, *Patrologia*, cci, 958–9; Matthew of Paris, *Chronica Majora*, ed. H. R. Luard, *Rerum britannicarum medii aevi scriptores*, 57, iii, London 1876, 488–9; Joinville, *Histoire de Saint Louis*, chapter lxxxix, in *Historiens et chroniqueurs du moyen âge*, ed. A. Pauphilet, Paris 1952, 307–10.

8   Nowell, 515, citing the French translation in *Collection des mémoires relatifs à l'histoire de France*, xxii, 47 f.; Latin text in his *Historia Orientalis*, i, 1062, in Bongars, *Gesta Dei per Francos*, Hanover 1611.

9   *The journey of William of Rubruck to the eastern parts of the world, 1253-55*, translated and edited by W. W. Rockhill, London 1900, 118, 222; *The texts and versions of John de Plano Carpini and William de Rubruquis*, ed. C. R. Beazley, London 1903, 170, 216, 324. Other versions speak of 400 assassins.

10 *The book of Ser Marco Polo*, trans. and ed. Sir Henry Yule, 3rd edn. revised by Henri Cordier, i, London 1903, chapters xxiii and xxiv, 139-43.

11 Ibn Muyassar, *Annales d'Egypte*, ed. H. Massé, Cairo 1919, 68; Al-Bondārī, abridged from 'Imād al-Dīn, *Histoire des Seldjoucides de l'Iraq*, ed. M. Th. Houtsma, *Recueil de textes relatifs à l'histoire des Seldjoucides*, i, Leiden 1889, 195; *Kitāb al-Radd 'alā'l-mulḥidīn*, ed. Muḥ. Taqī Dānishpazhūh in *Revue de la Faculté des Lettres, Université de Tabriz*, xvii/3 (1344 s), 312. In some versions of Marco Polo's narrative the actual word Assassin does not appear at all.

12 'Mémoire sur la dynastie des Assassins . . .', in *Mémoires de l'Institut Royal*, iv (1818), 1-85 (= *Mémoires d'histoire et de literature orientales*, Paris 1818, 322-403).

13 J. von Hammer, *Geschichte der Assassinen aus morgenländischen Quellen*, Stuttgart 1818; English translation, *The history of the Assassins*, trans. O. C. Wood, London 1835, 1-2, 217-18.

14 'Mémoire sur les Ismaélis et les Nosairis de la Syrie, addressé à M. Silvestre de Sacy par M. Rousseau . . .' in *Cahier xlii, Annales de Voyages*, xiv, Paris 1809-10, 271 ff.; further details in Lewis, 'Sources . . .', 477-9.

15 W. Monteith, 'Journal of a journey through Azerbijan and the shores of the Caspian', in *J.R.Geog.S.*, iii (1833) 15 ff.; J. Shiel, 'Itinerary from Tehrán to Alamút and Khurramabad in May 1837', *ibid.*, viii (1838), 430-4. See further L. Lockhart, 'Hasan-i-Sabbah and the Assassins' in *BSOAS*, v (1928-30), 689-96; W. Ivanow, 'Alamut', in *Geographical Journal*, lxxvii (1931), 38-45; Freya Stark, *The valleys of the Assassins*, London 1934; W. Ivanow, 'Some Ismaili strongholds in Persia', in *IC*, xii (1938), 383-92; *idem, Alamut and Lamasar*, Tehran 1960; P. Willey, *The castles of the Assassins*, London 1963; L. Lockhart and M. G. S. Hodgson, article 'Alamut', in *EI*(2); Manučehr Sutūdah, 'Qal'a-i Alamūt', in *Farhang-i Īrān zamīn*, iii (1334 s), 5-21.

16 *Annales des Voyages*, xiv (1818), 279; cit. St Guyard, *Un grand maître des Assassins . . .* repr. from *JA*, Paris 1877, 57-8.

17 J. B. Fraser, *Narrative of a journey into Khorassan*, London 1825, 376–7.

18 A full account of these events is given in an unpublished London University M.A. thesis by Zawahir Noorally, *The first Agha Khan and the British 1838–1868* ... presented April 1964. The Arnould judgement, published in Bombay in 1867, was reprinted in A. S. Picklay, *History of the Ismailis*, Bombay 1940, 113–70.

19 E. Griffini, 'Die jüngste ambrosianische Sammlung arabischer Handschriften', in *ZDMG*, 69 (1915), 63 f.

20 W. Ivanow, 'Notes sur l'"Ummu'l-Kitab" des Ismaëliens de l'Asie Centrale', in *REI* (1932), 418 f.; V. Minorsky, article 'Shughnān' in *EI(1)*; A. Bobrinskoy, *Sekta Isma'iliya v russkikh i bukharskikh predelakh*, Moscow 1902. For a brief account of a recent Soviet expedition to the Pamir see A. E. Bertel's, 'Otčet o rabote pamirskoy ekspeditsii ...' in *Izvestya Akad. Nauk Tadzhikskoy SSR*, 1962, 11–16.

Chapter 2 (pages 20–37)

The most comprehensive book on the Assassins is M. G. S. Hodgson, *The order of Assassins*, The Hague 1955. Though mainly concerned with the period after 1094, it includes some account of the earlier period. A shorter account of the religious development of the sect was written by W. Ivanow, *Brief survey of the evolution of Ismailism*, Leiden 1952. Mr Ivanow is the author of numerous books and articles dealing with particular aspects of Ismaili religion, literature and history. A history and description of the Ismailis, with special reference to India, are given in J. N. Hollister, *The Shī'a of India*, London 1953. A. S. Picklay, *History of the Ismailis*, Bombay 1940, is a popular account written by an Ismaili author for Ismaili readers. Among modern Arabic works, mention may be made of two general books by a Syrian Ismaili author Muṣṭafā Ghālib, a history, *Ta'rīkh al-da'wa al-Ismā'īliyya*, Damascus n.d., and a biographical dictionary, *A'lām al-Ismā'īliyya*, Beirut 1964, and of a general account by an Egyptian (non-Ismaili)scholar,Muḥammad Kāmil Ḥusayn,*Ṭā'ifat al-Ismā'īliyya*, Cairo 1959. Aspects of the early history of the sect have been examined by B. Lewis, *The origins of Ismā'īlism*, Cambridge 1940; W. Ivanow, *Ismaili tradition concerning the rise of the Fatimids*, London–Calcutta 1942, idem, *Studies in early Persian Ismailism*, Bombay 1955; W. Madelung, 'Fatimiden und Bahrainqarmaten', in *Der Islam*, xxxiv

(1958), 34–88; *idem*, 'Das Imamat in der frühen ismailitischen Lehre', *ibid.*, xxxvii (1961), 43–135; P. J. Vatikiotis, *The Fatimid theory of state*, Lahore 1957, and in numerous articles by Ivanow, Corbin, and S. M. Stern, listed by Pearson. There are many studies on Nāṣir-i Khusraw; that of A. E. Bertel's, *Nasir-i Khosrov i Ismailizm*, Moscow 1959, includes an extensive discussion of the historical background and significance of Ismailism in his time. Ghazālī's major polemic work against the Ismailis, written in 1094–95 for the Abbasid Caliph al-Mustaẓhir, was analysed by I. Goldziher, *Streitschrift des Gazālī gegen die Bāṭinijja-Sekte*, Leiden 1916. Another anti-Ismaili tract by Ghazālī was edited and translated into Turkish by Ahmed Ateş, 'Gazâlî'nin belini kıran deliller'i. Kitâb Ḳavāṣim al-Bāṭinīya', in *Ilâhiyat Fakültesi Dergisi* (Ankara), i–ii (1954), 23–54. Both of these are directed against the new doctrines of the Ismailis of his time. Ghazālī's attitudes to Ismailism are discussed by W. Montgomery Watt, *Muslim intellectual; a study of al-Ghazali*, Edinburgh 1963, 74–86.

On the place of the Ismailis within the larger framework of Islamic religion and history, reference may be made to H. Laoust, *Les schismes dans l'Islam*, Paris 1965; M. Guidi, 'Storia della religione dell' Islam', in P. Tacchi-Venturi, *Storia delle religioni*, ii, Turin 1936; A. Bausani, *Persia religiosa*, Milan 1959; W. Montgomery Watt, *Islam and the integration of society*, London 1961; B. Lewis, *The Arabs in history*, revised edn., London 1966, and to the relevant chapters in *L'Elaboration de l'Islam*, Paris 1961, and *The Cambridge Medieval History*, iv/1, new edn., Cambridge 1966.

1 H. Hamdani, 'Some unknown Ismāʿīli authors and their works', in *JRAS* (1933), 365.

Chapter 3 (pages 38–63)

The best account of Ḥasan-i Ṣabbāḥ (Arabic form, Al-Ḥasan ibn al-Ṣabbāḥ) is that given by Hodgson in *The order of Assassins* and, more briefly, in the article Ḥasan-i Ṣabbāḥ in *EI(2)*. There are earlier accounts in the general works on Ismailism, already mentioned, and in E. G. Browne, *A literary history of Persia from Firdawsi to Saʿdi*, London 1906, 201 ff. The struggle of Ḥasan-i Ṣabbāḥ against the Seljuqs is discussed, within the larger framework of the events of the time, by Ibrahim Kafesoğlu, in his book, in Turkish, on the Seljuq Empire in the time of Malikshāh (*Sultan Melikşah devrinde büyük Selçuklu imparatorluğu*, Istanbul 1953). A popular modern Ismaili presentation is given by Jawad al-Muscati, *Hasan bin Sabbah*, English translation by A. H. Hamdani, 2nd edn., Karachi 1958.

Ḥasan-i Ṣabbāḥ has also attracted the attention of modern Iranian and Arab scholars. Prof. Naṣrullah Falsafī has included an account of his career, with an edition of some documents, in his *Čand Maqāla*, Tehran 1342 s., 403–44, and Karīm Kashāvarz has published a semi-popular but documented biography, *Ḥasan-i Ṣabbāḥ*, Tehran 1344 s. There are two books in Arabic by Syrian Ismaili authors, 'Ārif Tāmir, *'Alā abwāb Alamūt*, Ḥarīṣa [1959], and Muṣṭafā Ghālib, *Al-Thā'ir al-Ḥimyarī al-Ḥasan ibn al-Ṣabbāḥ*, Beirut 1966. The first is an historical novel, the second a popular biography.

The most important single source for Ḥasan's life is his auto-biography, known as *Sarguzasht-i Sayyidnā* (the adventures of our lord). No copy has so far come to light, but the book was available to Persian historians of the Mongol period, who had access to the spoils of Alamūt and perhaps of other Ismaili fortresses and libraries. It was used, and in part quoted, by three Persian historians of that time, who wrote detailed accounts of Ḥasan-i Ṣabbāḥ and his succes-sors, based largely on captured Ismaili sources. The earliest and best known is 'Atā Malik Juvaynī (1226–83), whose history was edited by Mīrzā Muḥammad Qazvīnī (*Ta'rīkh-i Jahān-gushā*, 3 vols., London, 1912–37), and translated into English by J. A. Boyle (*The history of the world-conqueror*, 2 vols., Manchester 1958). The history of the Ismailis comes in the third volume of the text, second of the English translation. Part of the section dealing with the Ismailis was translated into French, from a Persian manuscript, by Charles Defrémery (*JA*, 5e série, viii, 1856, 353–87; xv, 1860, 130–210). Juvaynī describes how he found the Ismaili chronicles in the library of the captured fortress of Alamūt, copied what he thought of interest, and then destroyed them. He seems to follow his sources closely, taking care only to invert praise and blame, and to add the pious imprecations appropriate to an orthodox historian of a heterodox sect.

The second major source is a slightly later historian, Rashīd al-Dīn (*c*. 1247–1318), who included in his universal history a lengthy account of the Ismailis that is clearly based, directly or indirectly, on the same sources as were used by Juvaynī. Rashīd al-Dīn, however, obviously had fuller information available to him than appears in the extant text of Juvaynī. Despite some omissions, Rashīd al-Dīn seems to follow the text of the Ismaili sources more closely than did Juvaynī, and pre-serves many details omitted by his predecessor. Rashīd al-Dīn's history of the Ismailis has been known in manuscript for some time, and was used by Browne, Ivanow, Hodgson, and other scholars. The Persian text was published in 1958 (*Faṣlī aẓ Jāmiʿ al-tāvārīkh.. tārīkh-i firqa-i rafīqān va Ismāʿīliyyān-i Alamūt*, ed. Muḥammad Dabīr Siyāqī, Tehran 1337 s.) and republished, in another edition, in 1960 (*Jāmiʿ al-tavārīkh; qismat-i Ismāʿīliyyan.. *ed. Muḥammad Taqī Dānishpazhūh and Muḥ. Mudarrisī Zanjānī, Tehran 1338 s.). References are to the second of these editions. For earlier discussions of Rashīd al-Dīn see R. Levy, 'The account of the Ismaʿili doctrines in the *Jami' al-tawarikh* of Rashīd al-Dīn Fadlallah', in *JRAS* (1930), 509–36, and H. Bowen, 'The *sargudhasht-i sayyidnā*, the "Tale of the Three Schoolfellows", and the *wasaya* of the Niẓām al-Mulk', *ibid.*, (1931), 771–82. Scholars have been puzzled by the problem of how Rashīd al-Dīn could give a fuller and closer rendering of sources which Juvaynī alone had seen and then destroyed, and Bowen had suggested that Rashīd al-Dīn may have used an earlier and fuller draft which Juvaynī made and later discarded (cf. Hodgson, *Assassins*, 73 n. 34). The dilemma seems an artificial one; there were other Ismaili castles besides Alamūt, and it is reasonable to assume that some of them had libraries with copies of the sectarian histories. In addition to Juvaynī's work, which he obviously made use of, Rashīd al-Dīn may thus also have had direct access to copies of some of the books which Juvaynī had used.

In 1964 a third version came to light, by a contemporary of Rashīd al-Dīn, called Abu'l-Qāsim Kāshānī. The text has been published by Muḥ. Taqī Dānishpazhūh (*Tārīkh-i Ismāʿīliyya*, Tabriz 1343 s.). Kāshānī's text is very similar to that of Rashīd al-Dīn, and is probably related to it. It does, however, differ from it at some points, and contains details missing in both Rashīd al-Dīn and Juvaynī.

In addition to his autobiography, Ḥasan-i Ṣabbāḥ also appears to have written theological works. None of these are extant in their original form. Fragments, however, survive, in more or less modified versions, in later Ismaili literature (on which see W. Ivanow, *Ismaili literature: a bibliographical survey*, 2nd edn., Tehran 1963), and an important passage is cited, in an Arabic adaptation, by the twelfth-century Sunni theologian al-Shahrastānī (*Al-Milal wa'l-nihal*, ed. W. Cureton, London 1846, 150–2; ed. A. Fahmī Muḥammad, i, Cairo 1948, 339 ff; English trans. Hodgson, *Assassins*, 325–8).

Two documents, of disputed authenticity, are cited in later Persian collections, and purport to be an exchange of letters between Sultan

Malikshāh and Ḥasan-i Ṣabbāḥ. In the first the Sultan accuses Ḥasan of starting a new religion, misleading some ignorant mountain dwellers and renouncing and abusing the rightful Abbasid Caliph of Islam. He is to abandon these evil ways and return to Islam, failing which his castle will be razed to the ground and he and his followers destroyed. In a polite and elegantly expressed reply, Ḥasan, writing in a strongly autobiographical vein, defends his faith as the true Islam; the Abbasids are usurpers and evil-doers; and the true Caliph is the Fatimid Imam. He warns the Sultan against the false claims of the Abbasids, the intrigues of Niẓām al-Mulk, and the misdeeds of various oppressors, and urges him to take action against them; if he did not, another, more just ruler would arise and do it in his place. These texts, in slightly variant forms, were published by Mehmed Şerefuddin [Yaltkaya] in *Darülfünun Ilahiyat Fukültesi Mecmuası* (Istanbul), vii/4 (1926), 38–44, and again, independently, by Naṣrullah Falsafī in *Iṭṭilāʿāt-i Māhāna* (Tehran), 3/27, Khurdād 1329 s., 12–16 (reprinted in *idem, Čand maqāla*, Tehran 1342 s., 415–25). The authenticity of the letters is accepted by both editors and, more cautiously, by Osman Turan (*Selçuklular tarihi ve Türk-Islam medeniyeti*, Ankara 1965, 227–30), but is rejected by Kafesoğlu (*Sultan Melikşah ...*, 134–5, nn.). A comparison of the letter ascribed to Ḥasan with the known facts of his life on the one hand, and with extant specimens of Ismaili letter-writing on the other, would seem to confirm Kafesoğlu's doubts.

Accounts of Ḥasan-i Ṣabbāḥ and his successors at Alamūt by later Persian historians are based in the main on Juvaynī and Rashīd al-Dīn, with some additions of obviously legendary origin. There are however other sources of information. Much valuable information about the Ismailis can be gathered from the contemporary and near contemporary chronicles of the Seljuq Empire, including works in both Arabic and Persian, dealing with both general and local history. One of the best is the famous Arabic historian Ibn al-Athīr (1160–1234), whose history (*Al-Kāmil fiʾl-taʾrīkh*, 14 vols., ed. C. J. Tornberg, Leiden-Upsala, 1851–76; reprinted Cairo, 9 vols., 1348 ff.: both editions are cited), besides much relevant information, includes a short biography of Ḥasan-i Ṣabbāḥ, which is obviously independent of the *Sarguẕasht*. A fuller version of this biography, the source of which is unknown, is given by a later Egyptian chronicler (Maqrīzī, *al-Muqaffā*, Ms. Pertev Pasha 496, Istanbul). On the historians of this period in general see Claude Cahen, 'The historiography of the Seljuqid period', in B.

Lewis and P. M. Holt, edd., *Historians of the Middle East*, London 1962, 59–78. In addition to the literary sources, there is a growing body of archaeological evidence. Works dealing with the remains of the Ismaili castles in Iran are mentioned in n. 15 to ch. 1, above, and in n. 22 to ch. 3, below.

1   Rashīd al-Dīn, 97; Kāshānī, 120. Juvaynī, 187/667, has Ḥasan born in Rayy to which, according to other sources, he was taken as a child. This difference would seem to be due to careless abridgement by Juvaynī. According to Ibn al-Jawzī (d. 1201), Ḥasan came originally from Marv, and had served as secretary to the *ra'īs* 'Abd al-Razzāq ibn Bahrām when he was a young man (*Al-Muntaẓam*, ix, Hyderabad 1359, 121; *idem*, *Talbīs Iblīs*, Cairo 1928, 110; English translation by D. S. Margoliouth, 'The Devil's Delusion', in *IC*, ix, 1935, 555). In the alleged letter from Ḥasan to Malikshāh, he says that his father was a Shāfi 'ī Sunnī, and that he was brought up as such. This is one of several details that throw doubt on the authenticity of the letter. See Hodgson, 43; Falsafī, 406.

2   Juvaynī, 188–9/667–8; Rashīd al-Dīn, 97–9; Kāshānī, 120–3; Hodgson, 44–5. On Ibn 'Aṭṭāsh see *EI(2)* s.v. (by B. Lewis).

3   Rashīd al-Dīn, 110–2. On the three schoolfellows story see E. G. Browne, 'Yet more light on 'Umar-i Khayyām', in *JRAS* (1899), 409–16; H. Bowen, article cited above; Browne, *Lit. hist.*, 190–3; M. Th. Houtsma, *Recueil de textes relatifs à l'histoire des Seldjoucides*, ii, Leiden 1889, preface, pp. xiv–xv, n. 2; Hodgson, 137–8. Falsafī (406–10) defends the authenticity of the story. A late Egyptian source (Ibn al-Dawādārī, *Kanz al-durar*, vi, ed. Ṣalāḥ al-Dīn al-Munajjid, Cairo 1961, 494) says that Ḥasan-i Ṣabbāḥ was a fellow-student of Ghazālī. This would seem to be due to a misunderstanding.

4   Ibn al-Athīr, *anno* 494, x, 215–6/viii, 201; cf. *idem*, *anno* 427, ix, 304–5/viii, 11, and *anno* 487, x, 161/viii, 172–3. According to Ibn al-Athīr, Ḥasan travelled to Egypt disguised as a merchant. See further Maqrīzī, *Muqaffā*, s.v. al-Ḥasan ibn al-Ṣabbāḥ.

5   Ḥasan's own account of his journey to and from Egypt underlies the three versions of Juvaynī, 189–91/668–9, Rashīd al-Dīn, 99–103, and Kāshānī, 122–5. Cf. Hodgson, 45–7 (the error concerning the length of Ḥasan's stay in Egypt is corrected in the same author's article in *EI(2)*); Falsafī, 411–2. It is clear from Ḥasan's own account that he did not personally meet the Fatimid

Caliph, and that Ibn al-Athīr's story of such a meeting, and of the Caliph's deliberately ambiguous naming of his heir, is therefore untrue (see Asaf A. A. Fyzee, *Al-Hidāyatu'l-Āmirīya*, London–Calcutta 1938, 15). The apocryphal letter of Ḥasan to Malikshāh contains the curious assertion that the Commander of the Armies was incited against him by the Abbasid Caliph, and that he was saved from the plots of his enemies by the Imam himself.

6   Juvaynī, 190/669.

7   Ibn al-Faqīh, *Mukhtaṣar Kitāb al-Buldān*, ed. M. J. de Goeje, Leiden 1885, 283; cit. V. Minorsky, *La domination des Dailamites*, Paris 1932, 5.

8   Ibn al-Athīr, anno 494, x, 215/viii, 201.

9   Juvaynī, 193/669–70.

10   Juvaynī, 193–5/669–71; Rashīd al-Dīn, 103–5; Kāshānī, 125–8; Ibn al-Athīr, anno 494, x, 216/viii, 201–2; Hodgson, 48–50; Falsafī, 413–4.

11   Rashīd al-Dīn, 134; variant versions in Kāshānī, 154 and Juvaynī, 216/683. Characteristically, Juvaynī changes *da'vat* (mission) to *bid'at* (heretical innovation).

12   Juvaynī, 199/673–4; cf. Rashīd al-Dīn, 107; Kāshānī, 130.

13   Juvaynī, 208–9/679; Rashīd al-Dīn, 115–16; Kāshāni, 136–7.

14   Juvaynī, 200/674; Rashīd al-Dīn, 107–8; Kāshānī, 130–1; Ibn al-Athīr, anno 494, x, 217/viii, 202; Hodgson, 74.

15   Ibn al-Athīr, anno 494, x, 217/viii, 202; Hodgson, 76.

16   Ibn al-Jawzī, *Al-Muntaẓam*, ix, Hyderabad 1359 A.H., 120–1; *idem, Talbīs Iblīs*, Cairo 1928, 110 (English translation by D. S. Margoliouth in *IC*, ix, 1935, 555), Ibn al-Athīr, anno 494, x, 213/viii, 200–1; Hodgson, 47–8.

17   Juvaynī, 201–2/674–5; cf. Rashīd al-Dīn, 108–9; Kāshānī, 131; Hodgson, 74–5.

18   Rashīd al-Dīn, 110; cf. Juvaynī, 204/676–7 (and the editor's note on pp. 406–7 of the text); Kāshānī, 132–3; Ibn al-Athīr, anno 485, x, 137–8/viii, 161–2; M. Th. Houtsma, 'The death of Nizam al-Mulk and its consequences', in *Journal of Indian History*, iii (1924), 147–60; Hodgson, 75.

19   Persian text edited by Muḥ. Taqī Dānishpazhūh in *Revue de la Faculté des Lettres, Université de Tabriz*, xvii/3, 1344 s., 329. In this and the following issues Dr Dānishpazhūh has published a group of interesting sources, mostly polemical, concerning the Ismailis.

20 W. Ivanow, 'An Ismaili poem in praise of fidawis', in *JBBRAS*, xiv (1938), 63–72.

21 W. Ivanow, 'The organization of the Fatimid propaganda', in *JBBRAS*, xv (1939), 1–35; cf. the same author's remarks in the introductions to his editions of the *Divan* of Khaki Khorasani (Bombay 1933, 11) and of the *Haft bab of Abu Ishaq Quhistani* (Bombay 1959, 011–14). See further the articles 'dā'ī' (by H. G. S. Hodgson) and 'da'wa' (by M. Canard) in *EI*(2). The ranks are discussed by Naṣīr al-Dīn Ṭūsī, *The Rawdatu'l-Taslim, commonly called Tasawwurat*, ed. and translated by W. Ivanow, Bombay 1950, text 96–7, translation 143–4. For a modern Ismaili account, based on some early material, see Mian Bhai Mulla Abdul Husain, *Gulzari Daudi for the Bohras of India*, Ahmedabad n.d. [? 1920].

22 Juvaynī, 207–8/678–9; Rashīd al-Dīn, 116–20; Kāshānī, 137–41; Hodgson, 76 n. and 86–7. On the castle of Girdkūh see W. Ivanow, 'Some Ismaili strongholds in Persia', in *IC*, xii (1938), 392–6, and Manučehr Sutūdah, 'Qal 'a-i Girdkūh', in *Mihr*, viii (1331 s), 339–43 and 484–90.

23 The rise and fall of the Ismailis in Isfahan seem to have received little attention in the chronicle of Alamūt. Juvaynī has nothing to say on the subject; Rashīd al-Dīn (120 f.) and Kāshānī (142 f.) give brief accounts, which may be based on other, non-Ismaili sources. The episode is discussed in the general sources for the period, e.g. Ibn ar-Rāwandī, *Rāḥat-uṣ-Ṣudūr*, ed. Muḥ Iqbál, London 1921, 155–61; Ẓahīr al-Dīn Nīshāpūrī, *Saljūqnāme*, Tehran 1332 s., 39–42; Ibn al-Jawzī, *Muntaẓam*, ix, 150–1. Al-Bundārī, abridged from 'Imād al-Dīn, *Histoire des Seldjoucides de l'Iraq*, ed. M. Th. Houtsma, Leiden 1889, 90–2; Ibn al-Athīr, anno 494, x, 215–17/viii, 201–4; anno 500, x, 299–302/viii, 242–3, etc. Modern studies: Hodgson, 85–6, 88–9, 95–6; Lewis, 'Ibn 'Attāsh' in *EI*(2) s.v.; Muḥ. Mihryār, 'Shāhdiz Kujāst?', in *Revue de la Faculté des Lettres d'Isfahan*, i (1343/1965), 87–157.

24 Ibn al-Athīr, anno 494, x, 220/viii, 203.

25 Ibn al-Athīr, anno 497, x, 260/viii, 223.

26 Ibn al-Athīr, anno 494, x, 221/viii, 204.

27 Ibn al-Athīr, anno 500, x, 299/viii, 242. Ibn al-Athīr gives the fullest account of the siege.

28 Ibn al-Qalānisī, *History of Damascus*, ed. H. F. Amedroz, Beirut 1908, 153; French translation by R. Le Tourneau, *Damas de 1075 à 1154*, Damascus 1952, 68–9.

29 Juvaynī, 211/680; cf. Rashīd al-Dīn, 124–5; Kāshānī, 135–6; Ibn al-Qalānisī, 162 (= Le Tourneau, 83–4); al-Bundārī, 98–100; Ibn al-Athīr, *anno* 503, x, 335/viii, 259; Hodgson, 97.

30 Juvaynī, 207/678.

31 Juvaynī, 212/681; Rashīd al-Dīn, 126–32; Kāshānī, 141 ff.; Ibn al-Athīr, *anno* 511, x, 369–70/ix, 278.

32 Al-Bundārī, 147.

33 Juvaynī, 213–5/681–2; cf. Rashīd al-Dīn, 123; Kāshānī, 144. A Syrian Ismaili author tells the story of the dagger and the message in relation to Saladin.

34 Ibn al-Qalānisī, 203; English translation by H. A. R. Gibb, *The Damascus chronicle of the Crusades*, London 1932, 163.

35 Rashīd al-Dīn, 133, 137; cf. Kāshānī, 153, 156.

36 Ibn Muyassar, *Annales d'Egypte*, 65–6; cf. *ibid.* 68–9; Ibn al-Ṣayrafī, *Al-Ishāra ilā man nāla'l-wiẓāra*, ed. Ali Mukhlis, in *BIFAO*, xxv (1925), 49; S. M. Stern, 'The epistle of the Fatimid Caliph al-Āmir (al-Hidāya al-Āmiriyya) – its date and purpose', in *JRAS*, (1950), 20–31; Hodgson, 108–9.

37 Juvaynī, 215/682–3; cf. Rashīd al-Dīn, 133–4; Kāshānī, 153–4.

38 Ibn al-Athīr, *anno* 494, x, 216/viii, 201; Maqrīzī, *Muqaffā*, s.v. al-Ḥasan ibn al-Ṣabbāḥ.

39 Juvaynī, 210/680; cf. Rashīd al-Dīn, 124; Kāshānī, 145.

40 *ibid.*

41 On the autobiography, see the bibliographical note to this chapter, above. The abridgement of his treatise, called the four chapters, is given in an Arabic version by the twelfth-century heresiographer al-Shahrastānī, in his work *Al-Milal wa'l-niḥal*, cited above; English translation in Hodgson, 325–8.

Chapter 4 (pages 64–96)

Much of what was said above concerning the sources for the career of Ḥasan-i Ṣabbāḥ also applies to the history of the Ismailis in Persia in the period between his death and the Mongol conquest. Our main source is still the chronicles of Alamūt, as cited by Juvaynī, Rashīd al-Dīn, and Kāshānī. The extant literature of the Nizari Ismailis is mainly religious in content, but preserves some passages of historical interest. Additional information may be gathered from the general historical and other literature relating to the Seljuq, Khorazmian and Mongol periods, in Arabic and Persian. Very few of these works have as yet been translated into a European language. Apart from Professor Boyle's translation of Juvaynī, mention may be made of the following: Ch. Defrémery, 'Histoire des Seldjoucides' [the *Tārīkh-i Guzīda* of Ḥamdullah Mustawfī], in *JA*, xi (1848), 417–62; xii (1848), 259–79, 334–70; H. G. Raverty, *Ṭabakāt-i-Nāṣirī* [by Minhāj-i Sirāj Juzjānī], 2 vols., London 1881; O. Houdas, *Histoire du Sultan Djelal ed-Din Mankobirti* [by Muḥammad al-Nasawī], Paris 1895; E. G. Browne, *History of Ṭabaristan* [by Ibn Isfandiyār], London 1905. A group of coins from the Ismaili mint, struck in 542/1147–8, 548/1153–4, 551/1156–7, and 555/1160–1, was examined by P. Casanova, 'Monnaie des Assassins de Perse', in *Revue Numismatique*, 3ᵉ série, xi (1893), 343–52. A small Ismaili gold coin is preserved in the Istanbul Museum of Antiquities (E 175).

The basic monograph on the history of the Ismailis is that of Professor Hodgson, where earlier work by other scholars, notably W. Ivanow, is discussed. Briefer accounts will be found in the articles, 'Alamūt', 'Buzurg-ummīd', etc. in *EI(2)*. Particular aspects of Ismaili history have been discussed by Mme L. V. Stroyeva, ' "Den' voskresenya iz mertvıkh" i ego sotsial'naya sushčnost' ', in *Kratkiye Soobshčeniya Instituta Vostokovedeniya*, ınırviii (1960), 19–25, and 'Poslednii Khorezmshah i Ismailiti Alamuta', in *Issledovaniya po istorii kul'turı narodov vostoka: sbornik v čest' Akademika I. A. Orbeli*, Moscow–Leningrad 1960, 451–63. Some account of the Ismailis and their place in local history is given by H. L. Rabino di Borgomale, 'Les dynasties locales du Gîlân et du Daylam', in *JA*, ccxxxvii (1949), 301 ff, especially 314–6.

On the Seljuqs and their successors, reference may be made to the chapters by Claude Cahen in K. M. Setton (editor-in-chief), *A history of the Crusades*, vol. i, ed. M. W. Baldwin, Philadelphia 1955, chapter 5, and vol. ii, edd. R. L. Wolff and H. W. Hazard, 1962, chapters 19 and 21, and to relevant articles in *EI(1)* and *EI(2)*. Detailed works by Turkish, Persian and Arab scholars include: Osman Turan, *Selçuklular tarihi ve Türk-Islâm medeniyeti*, Ankara 1965; Mehmed Altay Köymen, *Büyük Selçuklu Imparatorluğu tarihi*, ii, *Ikinci Imparatorluk devri*, Ankara 1954; Ḥusayn Amīn, *Ta'rīkh al-'Irāq fī'l-'aṣr al-Saljūqī*, Baghdad 1965; Ibrahim Kafesoğlu, *Harezmşahler devleti tarihi*, Ankara 1956; 'Abbās Eghbāl, *Tārīkh-i mufaṣṣal-i Īrān...*, i, Tehran 1341 s.

1 Ibn al-Athīr, *anno* 520, x, 445/viii, 319; cf. Ibn Funduq Bayhaqī,

Tārīkh-i Bayhaq, ed. Aḥmad Bahmanyār, Tehran, n.d., 271, 276; Köymen, 151–6; Hodgson, 101–2.

2   Ibn al-Athīr, *anno* 521, x, 456/viii, 325; cf. Khwāndamīr, *Dastūr al-vuzarā*, Tehran 1317, 198; Nāṣir al-Dīn Munshī Kirmānī, *Nasā'im al-ashār*, ed. Jalāl al-Dīn Muḥaddith, Tehran 1959, 64–9; 'Abbās Eghbāl, *Vazārat dar 'ahd-i salāṭīn-i buzurg-i Saljūqī*, Tehran 1338 s., 254–60.

3   Rashīd al-Dīn, 138; Kāshānī, 158. The construction of Maymūndiz is not mentioned by Juvaynī. For a detailed description of the site see Willey, *The castles of the Assassins*, 158 ff.

4   *Tārīkh-i Sīstān*, ed. Bahār, Tehran 1935, 391.

5   Rashīd al-Dīn, 140; Kāshānī, 159.

6   Juvaynī, 220–1/685; cf. Rashīd al-Dīn, 141–2; Kāshānī, 164–5; Hodgson, 104.

7   Rashīd al-Dīn, 142; Kāshānī, 165; Hodgson, 103.

8   Rashīd al-Dīn, 141; Kāshānī, 160–4 (a very full account); Hodgson, 103.

9   Juvaynī, 221/685.

10 Rashīd al-Dīn, 146; Kāshānī, 168.

11 Rashīd al-Dīn, 146–7; Kāshānī, 168–9; Ibn al-Athīr, *anno* 532, xi, 40–1/viii, 362; Köymen, 304; Kafesoğlu, 26; Hodgson, 143–4.

12 Rashīd al-Dīn, 155; Kāshānī, 176; Ibn al-Athīr, *anno* 541, xi, 76–7/ix, 15; Hodgson, 145–6.

13 Juvaynī, 222–4/686–7; cf. Rashīd al-Dīn, 162–4; Kāshānī, 183–4.

14 Abū Ishāq Quhistānī, *Haft bāb*, ed. and trans. by W. Ivanow, Bombay 1959, 41; cf. W. Ivanow, *Kalām-i Pīr*, Bombay 1935, 60–1 and 115–7; Juvaynī, 226–30/668–91; Rashīd al-Dīn, 164 ff.; Kāshānī, 184 ff.; other Ismaili accounts in the *Haft bāb-i Bābā Sayyidna* (ed. Ivanow in *Two early Ismaili treatises*, Bombay 1933, English translation, with commentary, in Hodgson, *Assassins*, 279–324) and in Ṭūsī's *Rawḍat al-taslīm* (index). Discussions in Hodgson, 148–57; Bausani, *Persia religiosa*, 211–2; H. Corbin and Moh. Mo'in, edd., Nasir-i Khosrow, *Kitab-e Jami' al-hikmatain*, Tehran–Paris 1953, introduction, 22–5; Stroyeva, 'Den' voskresenya . . .', *loc.cit.* (in bibliographical note above).

15 Juvaynī, 230/691; cf. Rashīd al-Dīn, 166; Kāshānī, 186.

16 Juvaynī, 237–8/695–6; cf. Rashīd al-Dīn, 168–9; Kāshānī, 188. Similar doctrines are attributed to the strangler sects in the eighth century. See above pp. 26 and 128.

17 Rashīd al-Dīn, 169; cf. Juvaynī, 238/696; Kāshānī, 188 (with some extracts from pious Ismaili eulogies of Ḥasan).

18 Juvaynī, 239/697; cf. Rashīd al-Dīn, 169–70; Kāshānī, 191; Hodgson, 157–9.

19 Rashīd al-Dīn, 170–3; cf. Kāshānī, 192–4; Hodgson, 183.

20 P. Kraus, 'Les "Controverses" de Fakhr al-Dīn Rāzī', in *BIE*, xix (1936–7), 206 ff. (English version in *IC*, xii, 1938, 146 ff.).

21 Juvaynī, 241–4/698–701; cf. Rashīd al-Dīn, 174 ff.; Kāshānī, 198 ff.; Hodgson, 217 ff.

22 Juvaynī, 247/702–3; Kāshānī, 199; Hodgson, 224–5.

23 Juvaynī, 248/703; cf. Rashīd al-Dīn, 177–8; Kāshānī, 200–1.

24 Juvaynī, 249/703—4; cf. Rashīd al-Dīn, 178; Kāshānī, 201.

25 Hammer, *History of the Assassins*, 154–5.

26 Naṣīr al-Dīn Ṭūsī, *Rawḍat al-taslīm*, text, 49, translation, 67–8; cf. Hodgson, 229–31.

27 Juvaynī, 249–53/704–7; cf. Rashīd al-Dīn, 179 ff.; Kāshānī, 201 ff.

28 Mohammed en-Nesawi [Nasawī], *Histoire du Sultan Djelal ed-Dīn Munkubirti*, ed. O. Houdas, Paris 1891, 132–4; French translation, Paris 1895, 220–3. A nearly contemporary Persian translation was edited by Prof. Mujtabā Minovi, *Sīrat-e Jelāloddīn*, Tehran 1965, 163–6.

29 Nasawī, Arabic text, 214–5; French translation, 358–9; Persian text, 232–3.

30 Rashīd al-Dīn, 181; cf. Kāshānī, 205; Hodgson, 257.

31 Juvaynī, 253–6/707–9; cf. Rashīd al-Dīn, 182–4; Kāshānī, 205–6.

32 Minhāj-i Sirāj Juzjānī, *Ṭabaqāt-i Nāṣirī*, ed. Abdul Hai Habibi, 2nd edn., i, Kabul 1964, 182–3; English trans. H. G. Raverty, ii, 1197–8.

33 Juvaynī, 260/712–3; cf. Rashīd al-Dīn, 185–6; Kāshānī, 207.

34 Juvaynī, 265/716; cf. Rashīd al-Dīn, 189; Kāshānī, 209.

35 Juvaynī, 267/717; cf. Rashīd al-Dīn, 190; Kāshānī, 210.

36 Rashīd al-Dīn, 192. Kāshānī, 213, calls her a Turk; Juvaynī, 274/722 goes further, and makes her a low-class Turk. On this point see Prof. Boyle's note on p. 722 of his translation. On the camel story also Juvaynī and Kāshānī agree on a version slightly different from that of Rashīd al-Dīn (213).

37 Juvaynī, 136/636–7.

38 Juvaynī, 277/724–5; cf. Rashīd al-Dīn, 194; Kāshānī, 215.

39 Juvaynī, 139–42/639–40.
40 Juvaynī, 278/725; cf. Rashīd al-Dīn, 194–5; Kāshānī, 215. The final quotation is from the Qur'ān, vi, 116.

Chapter 5 (pages 97–124)

Much has been written about the history of the Assassins in Syria. The most recent general accounts will be found in the relevant sections of Hodgson's *Assassins* and in B. Lewis, 'The Ismā'īlites and the Assassins', Chapter 4 of K. M. Setton (editor-in-chief), *A history of the Crusades*, i, ed. M. W. Baldwin, *The first hundred years*, Philadelphia 1955, 99–132; where full references to sources are given. Earlier literature is surveyed in B. Lewis, 'The sources for the history of the Syrian Assassins', in *Speculum*, xxvii (1952), 475–89. Among older studies, two articles by Ch. Defrémery, 'Nouvelles recherches sur les Ismaéliens ou Bathiniens de Syrie', in *JA*, 5ᵉ série, iii (1854), 373–421 and v (1855), 5–76, still deserve attention. More recent work includes B. Lewis, 'Saladin and the Assassins', in *BSOAS*, xv (1953), 239–45; J. J. Saunders, *Aspects of the Crusades*, Christchurch, New Zealand, 1962, Chapter iii (The role of the Assassins), 22–7; and an unpublished thesis, Nasseh Ahmad Mirza, *The Syrian Ismā'īlīs at the time of the Crusades*, Ph.D. Durham, 1963.

Of late, Syrian Ismaili authors have begun to publish both texts and studies. So far the texts have all been of primarily doctrinal content, and offer little of direct historical interest. Some information may be gathered from a modern biographical dictionary, based in part on traditional materials, by Muṣṭafā Ghālib, *A'lām al-Ismā'īliyya*, Beirut 1964, and from a number of articles by 'Ārif Tāmir in Arabic journals, including some early evidence: 'Sinān Rāshid al-Dīn aw Shaykh al-jabal', in *Al-Adīb*, May 1953, 43–5; 'Al-Amīr Mazyad al-Hillī al-Asadī, Shā'ir Sinān Shaykh al-jabal', in *Al-Adīb*, August 1953, 53–6; 'Al-Shā'ir al-Maghmūr: al-Amīr Mazyad al-Ḥilli al-Asadī', in *Al-Ḥikma*, January 1954, 49–55; 'Al-Firqa al-Ismā'īliyya al-Bāṭiniyya al-Sūriyya', in *Al-Ḥikma*, February 1954, 37–40; 'Al-Fatra al-mansiyya min ta'rīkh al-Ismā'īliyyīn al-Sūriyyīn', in *Al-Ḥikma*, July 1954, 10–13; 'Ṣafaḥāt aghfalahā al-ta'rīkh 'an al-firqa al-Ismā'īliyya al-Sūriyya', in *Al-Ḥikma*, September 1954, 39–41; 'Furū' al-shajara al-Ismā'īliyya al-imāmiyya', in *Al-Mashriq*, (1957), 581–612 (including the text of a letter from Jalāl al-Dīn Ḥasan, lord of Alamūt, to the Ismailis in Syria – 601–3). Mr Tāmir has also published an article in English, 'Bahram b.

Musa: the supreme Isma'ili agent', in *Ismaili News* (Uganda), 21
March 1954, and an Arabic historical novel, *Sinān wa-Ṣalāḥ al-Dīn*,
Beirut 1956, as well as a considerable number of texts.

From what has come to light so far, it would seem that the Ismailis
of Syria preserved no histories comparable with the chronicles of
Alamūt cited by Juvaynī and other Persian historians. An Ismaili biography of Sinān, the most important of the Syrian chiefs, is late,
hagiographic, and of limited historical value. The text was published,
with French translation, by S. Guyard, 'Un grand maître des Assassins
au temps de Saladin', in *JA*, 7ᵉ série, ix (1877), 324–489, and republished by Mehmed Şerefüddin [Yaltkaya] in *Darülfünun Ilahiyat
Fakültesi Mecmuast*, ii/7 (Istanbul 1928), 45–71. Some evidence
of Ismaili provenance is cited in the life of Sinān, included in
Kamāl al-Dīn Ibn al-'Adīm's unpublished biographical dictionary of
Aleppo; text, with translation and commentary, in B. Lewis, 'Kamāl
al-Dīn's biography of Rāshid al-Dīn Sinān', in *Arabica*, xiii (1966).

Apart from a few such fragmentary survivals, and the local inscriptions (on which see M. van Berchem, 'Epigraphie des Assassins
de Syrie', in *JA*, 9ᵉ série, ix (1897), 453–501), the historian of the
Syrian Assassins must rely on the general sources for the history of
Syria in the period.

1   Arabic text in B. Lewis, 'Three biographies from Kamāl al-Dīn',
    in *Mélanges Fuad Köprülü*, Istanbul 1953, 336.

2   Kamāl al-Dīn Ibn al-'Adim, *Zubdat al-ḥalab min ta'rīkh Ḥalab*,
    ed. Sāmī Dahān, ii, Damascus 1954, 532–3.

3   Ibn al-Qalānisī, *History of Damascus*, ed. H. F. Amedroz, Beirut
    1908, 215; English translation by H. A. R. Gibb, *The Damascus
    chronicle of the Crusades*, London 1932, 179.

4   Kamāl al-Dīn, *Zubda*, ii, 235.

5   Ibn al-Qalānisī, 221; English trans., 187–8.

6   Ibn al-Qalānisī, 223; English trans., 193.

7   Rashīd al-Dīn, 145; Kāshānī, 167. Both give the date of the murder
    as 524 A.H. The Syrian sources agree that Buri was attacked in
    525 and died in 526 A.H. According to one report his attackers
    used poisoned daggers. The use of poison is not confirmed by the
    contemporary sources, and seems very unlikely.

8   B. Lewis, 'Kamāl al-Dīn's biography of Rāshid al-Dīn Sinān'
    231–2.

9   B. Lewis, 'Kamāl al-Dīn's biography ...', 230.

10 Kamāl al-Dīn, *Zubda*, Ms. Paris, Arabe 1666, fol. 193b ff.

11 Lewis, 'Kamāl al-Dīn's biography . . .', 231.

12 *ibid.*, 10–11. The first of 'the Bee' and the last of 'Ṣād' are verses from the Qur'ān. They read: 'The decree of God has come, seek not to hasten it; glory be to Him and exalted be He away from all that they associate (with Him)' (xvi.1). 'Ye shall surely know the story of it after a while' (xxxviii, 88).

13 *ibid.*, 12–13.

14 Muḥammad al-Ḥamawī, *Al-Ta'rīkh al-Manṣūrī*, ed. P. A. Gryaznevič, Moscow 1960, fols. 164 a and b, 166b–167a, 170b.

15 Joinville, chapter lxxxix, 307.

16 Maqrīzī, *Kitāb al-Sulūk*, ed. M. M. Ziyāda, i, Cairo 1943, 543; French translation E. Quatremère, *Histoire des sultans mamlouks*, i/2, Paris 1837, 245; 'Aynī, in *RHC, historiens orientaux*, ii/a, Paris 1887, 223. See further Defrémery, 'Nouvelles recherches . . .', 50–1.

17 Ibn Baṭṭūṭa, *Voyages*, ed. and French trans. by Ch. Defrémery and B. R. Sanguinetti, i, Paris 1853, 166–7; cf. English translation by H. A. R. Gibb, *The travels of Ibn Battuta*, i, Cambridge 1958, 106.

18 Registers for the district of Maṣyāf, in the province of Ḥamā, and for the group of districts called *Qilā' al-da'wa* (Castles of the mission) in the province of Tripoli. These consist of Khawābī, Kahf, 'Ulayqa, Qadmūs, and Manīqa. A study of these registers is in progress. On more recent history see N. N. Lewis, 'The Isma'ilis of Syria today', in *RCASJ*, xxxix (1952), 69–77.

Chapter 6 (pages 125–140)

Some discussion of the methods, purposes, and significance of the Ismailis will be found in the works already cited, especially those of Hodgson and Bertel's. Briefer characterizations are given in articles by D. S. Margoliouth ('Assassins' in *Hastings Encyclopaedia of Religion and Ethics*) and, more recently, by R. Gelpke ('Der Geheimbund von Alamut – Legende und Wirklichkeit', in *Antaios*, viii, 1966, 269–93). An important aspect of the religious evolution of Ismailism is discussed by Henry Corbin, 'De la gnose antique à la gnose ismaélienne', in *Convegno di scienze morali storiche e filologiche 1956: Oriente ed Occidente nel medio evo*, Rome 1957, 105–46.

Muslim views on the problems of authority and of tyranny have been discussed by Miss Ann K. S. Lambton ('The problem of the unrighteous ruler', in *International Islamic Colloquium*, Lahore 1960, 61–3; *eadem*, 'Quis custodiet custodes: some reflections on the Persian theory of government', in *SI*, v, 1956, 125–48; vi, 1956, 125–46; 'Justice in the medieval Persian theory of kingship', in *SI*, xvii, 1962, 91–119); by H. A. R. Gibb (*Studies on the civilization of Islam*, London 1962, 141 ff.); by G. E. von Grunebaum (*Islam: essays in the nature and growth of a cultural tradition*, London 1955, 127–40, and *Medieval Islam*, 2nd edn., Chicago 1953, 142–69). There appears to be no study of assassination as such, but it may be noted that a ninth-century author in Baghdad wrote a history of the murders and assassinations of prominent people (Muḥammad ibn Ḥabīb, *Asmā' al-mughtālīn min al-ashrāf*, ed. 'Abd al-Salām Hārūn, in *Nawādir al-makhṭuṭāt*, 6–7, Cairo 1954–5). The Muslim law on killing – both as a crime and as a punishment – is discussed by J. Schacht, article 'Ḳatl' in *EI(1)*.

The most recent treatment of Muslim messianism is that of Emanuel Sarkisyanz (*Russland und der Messianismus des Orients*, Tübingen 1955, 223 ff.). Earlier discussions include: J. Darmesteter, *Le Mahdi*, Paris 1885; E. Blochet, *Le Messianisme dans l'hétérodoxie musulmane*, Paris 1903; D. S. Margoliouth, 'Mahdī', in *Hastings Encyclopaedia of Religion and Ethics*; C. Snouck Hurgronje, 'Der Mahdi', in *Verspreide Geschriften*, i, Bonn 1923, 147–81; D. B. MacDonald, 'Al-Mahdī', in *EI(1)*.

The men's societies in Islam – guilds, train-bands, religious orders, etc. – have formed the subject of an extensive literature, of which a few examples, dealing with different aspects, must suffice: Cl. Cahen, 'Mouvements populaires et autonomisme urbain dans l'Asie musulmane du moyen âge', in *Arabica*, v (1958), 225–50; vi (1959), 25–56, 223–65; H. J. Kissling, 'Die islamischen Derwischorden', in *Zeitschrift für Religions – und Geistesgeschichte*, xii (1960), 1–16; *EI(2)*, articles ''Ayyār' (by F. Taeschner), 'Darwīsh' (by D. B. MacDonald) and 'Futuwwa' by C. Cahen and F. Taeschner).

1 For the evidence in support of this interpretation of the first civil war in Islam, see Laura Veccia Vaglieri, 'Il conflitto 'Alī-Muʻāwiya e la secessione kharigita . . .', in *Annali dell' Istituto Universitario Orientale di Napoli*, n.s. iv (1952), 1–94.
2 On an apparent exception, see Hodgson, 114, n. 43.
3 Above p. 4.
4 G. van Vloten, 'Worgers in Islam', in *Feestbundel van Taal-Letter-, Geschied- en Aardrijkskundige Bijdragen . . . aan Dr P. J.*

Veth ... Leiden, 1894, 57–63; I. Friedlaender, 'The heterodoxies of the Shi'ites', in *JAOS*, xxviii (1907), 62–4; xxix (1908), 92–5; Laoust, *Schismes*, 33–4.

5   W. Ivanow, 'An Ismaili poem in praise of Fidawis', in *JBBRAS*, xiv (1938), 71.

6   J. B. S. Hardman, 'Terrorism', in *Encyclopaedia of the Social Sciences*.

7   Joinville, Chapter lxxxix, 307.

8   Ḥamdullah Mustawfī, *Tārīkh-i Guzīda*, ed. E. G. Browne, London–Leiden 1910, 455–6; French trans. by Ch. Defrémery, in *JA*, 4ᵉ sér., xii (1848), 275.

9   These various economic interpretations are critically examined by A. E. Bertel's, *Nasir-i Khosrov i Ismailizm*, especially 142 ff., where the Russian literature is cited. A more recent view is given in Mme Stroeya's article, already mentioned. Barthold gave a brief statement of his views in an article published in German, 'Die persische Šuʿūbīja und die moderne Wissenschaft', in *Zeitschrift für Assyriologie*, xxvi (1911), 249–66.

The Assassins